PUNCH NEEDLE TOYS

**20 toys to make
with punch needle
embroidery**

Caro Bello

DAVID & CHARLES

www.davidandcharles.com

CONTENTS

INTRODUCTION

Welcome to the wonderful world of punch needle!

Punch needle is an ancient embroidery technique traditionally used for making rugs and tapestries. But did you know that you can also use this technique for modern applications, such as toys and dolls?

With the punch needle technique, you can make flat toys seem three-dimensional, due to the great variety of textures that you can create.

You don't need to be an expert in sewing or making toys. By the time you finish this book, you will know exactly what to do and can enjoy making the cute animals you see here your very own.

WHAT IS PUNCH NEEDLE?

Punch needle is quite different from traditional embroidery. At first glance, it may look like tapestry or loom techniques. Punch needle, however, needs to be worked on a foundation fabric, so it is categorized as embroidery.

There are three distinct features of the punch needle technique that help us to understand it better.

Unique needle

The technique is carried out with a special needle, similar to an awl. There are many kinds of punch needles, but the needle part is hollow with a hole in one side.

Double-sided

The punch needle produces embroidery with two very different looks. On the 'front' side of the fabric the stitches look flat, while on the 'back' a loop is formed for each stitch. We can therefore show off our embroidery on the flat side or on the looped side, and even combine both effects on the same side.

No knots

Finally, the aspect of the technique that is the worst nightmare for beginners: we don't tie knots! Therefore, if we do not embroider correctly, the stitches will come loose – but we are going to do it correctly!

There are two reasons stitches come loose or do not sit well in the fabric:

- the wrong yarn and fabric are being used (see Tools & Materials introduction and Yarn and Fabric sections).
- the needle movements are not being worked correctly (see Using the Needle, under The four golden rules).

Don't worry – I will show you how to avoid these things happening.

TOOLS & MATERIALS

For the punch needle technique to work, it is essential to combine the needle, fabric and yarn correctly so that the stitches do not come loose.

The size of the hole that the needle will make in the fabric must match the thickness of the yarn, so that the stitch will be held in place. If the yarn is thinner than the hole, the stitch will be loose and fall out of the fabric.

Equally, the fabric must suit the thickness of the needle and yarn. For example, if the fabric is very stiff or closely woven and the diameter of the needle is thick, the needle will not be able to pierce the fabric easily,

possibly breaking the threads in the fabric as you sew. If the fabric is an open weave and your needle and yarn are thinner than the hole they are going into, again, the fabric won't hold the yarn, so the stitches will come loose.

The table is a general guide to give an idea of how to achieve the correct combinations of needle, yarn and fabric, but yarns and fabrics do vary, so experiment to get the result you want.

PUNCH NEEDLES		YARN			FABRIC	
Thickness	Diameter	Weights (UK)	Weights (US)	Knitting needle sizes Metric (US)	Types of fabric	Examples
Extra-fine	1mm	1 ply	0 lace	1.5–2.25mm (000–1)	Compact- or extra close-weave fabrics	Denim, cotton, silk, rayon, poplin
Extra-fine	1.5mm	Cobweb, embroidery thread	1 super fine, light fingering, sock, baby	2.25–3.25mm (1–3)	Compact- or extra close-weave fabrics	Denim, cotton, silk, rayon, poplin
Fine	2mm	4 ply, baby	2 fine, fingering, sport, sock, baby	3.25–3.75mm (3–5)	Compact- or extra close-weave fabrics	Denim, cotton, silk, rayon, poplin
Medium	2.5mm	DK	3 light, DK, light worsted	3.75–4.5mm (5–7)	Fine-weft fabric: more than 5 holes per cm (⅜in)	Panama, linen, weaver's cloth, osnaburg, evenweave
Medium	3mm	Aran	4 medium, worsted, Aran, Afghan	4.5–5.5mm (7–9)	Fine-weft fabric: more than 5 holes per cm (⅜in)	Panama, linen, weaver's cloth, osnaburg, evenweave
Thick	4mm	Chunky	5 bulky, craft, rug	5.5–8mm (9–11)	Semi-open-weave fabric: 5 holes per cm (⅜in)	Fine- or close-weave burlap or jute, monk's cloth, panama
Extra-thick	5–6mm	Super chunky	6 super bulky, roving	8–12mm (11–17)	Open weave fabric: fewer than 5 holes per cm (⅜in)	Rustic burlap or jute, monk's cloth, primitive backing, hessian backing

NEEDLES

There is a wide variety of punch needles – different brands, colours and shapes. To identify them easily, regardless of brand or model, they are described according to their thickness (the diameter of the metal tip in mm) – extra-fine, fine, medium, thick and extra-thick. The different thicknesses are available in different lengths, sometimes assigned a number. The length determines what size the loops will be. The needles are also available in several different types.

Adjustable needles

- The needle point can be moved up or down to the desired length for each project.
- The longer the metal tip of the needle, the longer the loop will be.
- In this way, a variety of effects can be achieved with just one needle.
- Available in all thicknesses and lengths.
- They only come without a slot.

Non-adjustable needles

- These are the most basic needles, as the length of the metal tip cannot be changed.
- Available in all thicknesses and lengths.
- Available with or without a slot.

Slotless needles

- The classic needles.
- They do not have a slot along the handle, so a threader is needed to thread them.
- Available in all thicknesses.
- Can be non-adjustable or adjustable.

Slotted needles

- These are my favourite!
- They have a long slot along the handle, so are easy to thread.
- They are very ergonomic.
- The open tip punches into the fabric easily.
- They only come in extra-thick, thick and medium, but in a variety of lengths.
- They are not adjustable.

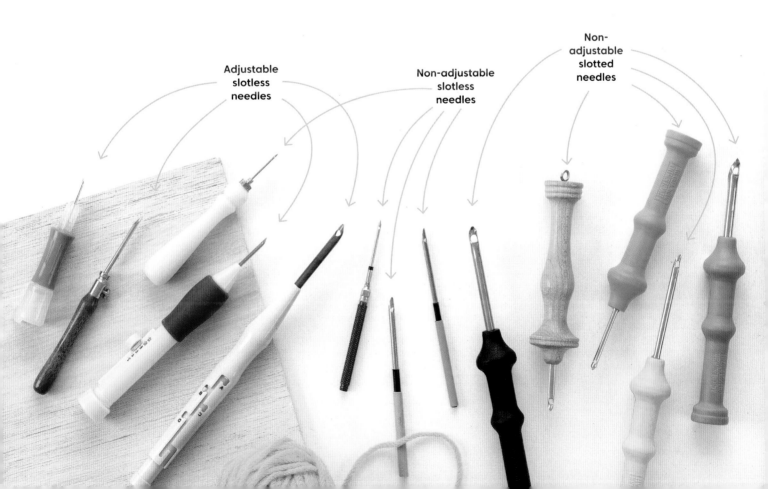

Adjustable slotless needles

Non-adjustable slotless needles

Non-adjustable slotted needles

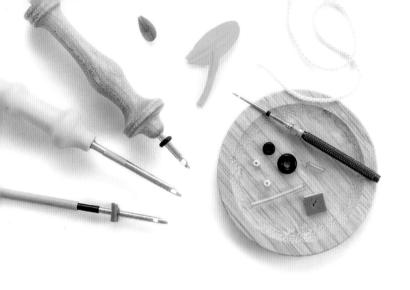

One way to vary the length of the loops with a non-adjustable needle is by adding a 'stop' – a ring or sleeve that is placed on the tip of the needle. This makes the loop shorter than the one usually generated by that length of needle. You can add one or more stops, but always keep in mind that the loop can only be made shorter this way, not longer.

Stops can be made from:

- cut straws
- rubber O rings, such as are used for taps
- serum hose
- plastic beads
- soft foam rubber cut-outs

YARN

To find which punch needle will be best for a yarn you want to use, be guided by the size of knitting needles that are recommended for use with the yarn. The size is usually given next to a crossed needles icon on the label for the yarn. From the table in Tools & Materials, you can see that each thickness of punch needle can be used for any of a range of comparable knitting needle sizes. For example, if the yarn label says '6mm', a thick punch needle will be needed as it is recommended for 5.5–8mm (9–11 US) knitting needles.

Essentially, the yarn has to be almost the same thickness as the diameter of the needle. If it is much thinner or much thicker, use either a different thickness of needle or a different thickness of yarn.

When threading the needle, the yarn should run easily into the needle, but take up all the space. It should not get stuck or be loose inside the needle.

Any thread or yarn can be used, as long as it is the right thickness for the needle, but the easiest to use are wool and acrylic yarns. Their 'fuzz' helps them to grip the fabric better than cotton, which can slip around easily.

If the stitches come loose, do the threading test. The yarn should neither get stuck nor slip through too easily but still slide.

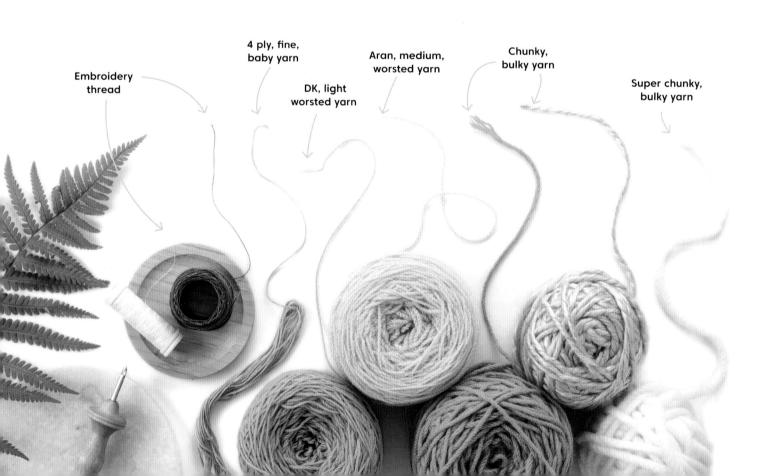

Embroidery thread

4 ply, fine, baby yarn

DK, light worsted yarn

Aran, medium, worsted yarn

Chunky, bulky yarn

Super chunky, bulky yarn

FABRIC

The fabric serves as a support for the stitches and gives structure to the embroidery. It helps to keep each stitch fixed in place, so that the loops do not move.

The ideal fabrics for this technique are ones with a simple weave of single horizontal threads (weft) crossing single vertical threads (warp) in a grid format. There are fabrics that are very tightly woven with thick threads, while others have a more open weave, so you can see through them, making them more flexible than the thicker fabrics. This means that you can't use just any fabric. The ideal one for your project will depend on the needle that you want to work with.

Most of the fabrics that are best for punch needle embroidery are those used for interior decoration (curtains, upholstery, crafts), not dressmaking.

A top tip for finding out whether or not a fabric is suitable for a needle and yarn you have in mind is to count the holes in 1cm (⅜in). To make this easier, take a small piece of stiff, thin cardboard and cut out a 1 x 1cm (⅜ x ⅜in) window in the centre. As a rule of thumb, for:

- 5 holes per cm (⅜in), use medium thickness needles (2.5 or 3mm)

- more than 5 holes per cm (⅜in, which will mean that the holes are smaller), use fine needles (2mm)

- fewer than 5 holes per cm (⅜in, which will mean that the holes are bigger), use thick and extra-thick needles (4 or 6mm).

Note that there are fabrics that appear to be tightly woven but easily adapt to thicker needles being used with them. For this reason, I always recommend seeing the fabrics in person rather than buying them online.

When punching, the fabric should offer some resistance as the needle first contacts it, but then give way as you pierce it. If the needle goes through the fabric too easily, it will not work well, because the fabric will lack the necessary strength to hold the stitches in place and they will come loose. Conversely, if you need to use force to punch the fabric, it is likely that threads in the fabric will snap, spoiling your work.

For most of the projects in this book, I have used both medium and fine needles, to create texture. I have used the recommended yarns for each needle on panama fabric, but any fabric with 5 or 6 holes per cm (⅜in) would work just as well.

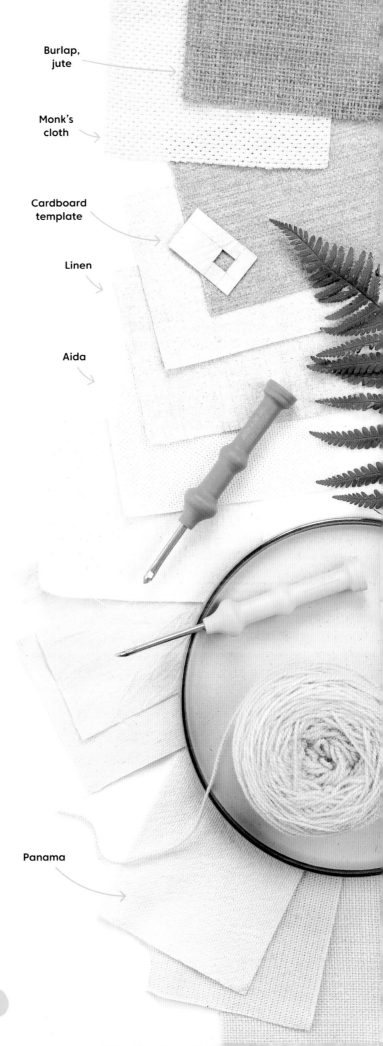

Burlap, jute

Monk's cloth

Cardboard template

Linen

Aida

Panama

EMBROIDERY HOOPS & FRAMES

Their function is to stretch the fabric evenly so that it is comfortable to embroider. Unlike traditional embroidery, the hoops or frames must hold the fabric tightly, so the weft can open up, making it easier to punch the needle through the holes. Hoops, therefore, must be strong, to withstand the movements made with the needle without falling apart.

Gripper strip frame

This is my favourite design! The gripper strips are similar to hook-and-loop tape but are made from metal. They have small spikes to 'grip' the fabric, hence their name. This is the simplest method of placing and stretching fabric for punch needle embroidery.

You can purchase these frames ready made or make one yourself. The base is a wooden frame with rounded outer edges to which the gripper strips are attached, wrapping round the top face and outer edge of each side of the frame. It is important that the metal 'hairs' on the gripper strips point towards the outer edges of the frame on each side.

The only disadvantage is that ready-made gripper strip frames are expensive and not readily available, but you can either make one or choose from the cheaper, easier-to-find options listed here.

Q-Snap frame

These frames are made from plastic tubes that clip together. They are very practical, as they are both light and can be dismantled and stored away when not in use. They come in square and rectangular formats.

Hoop

I recommend the hoops that come with an internal groove or ridging, as they will hold the fabric in place better than those without. Do not use either bamboo or very fine wooden hoops, as they are not strong enough for punch needle.

Wooden frame

Simply wrap the fabric around the frame and secure it to the back with staples, stretching it as you go.

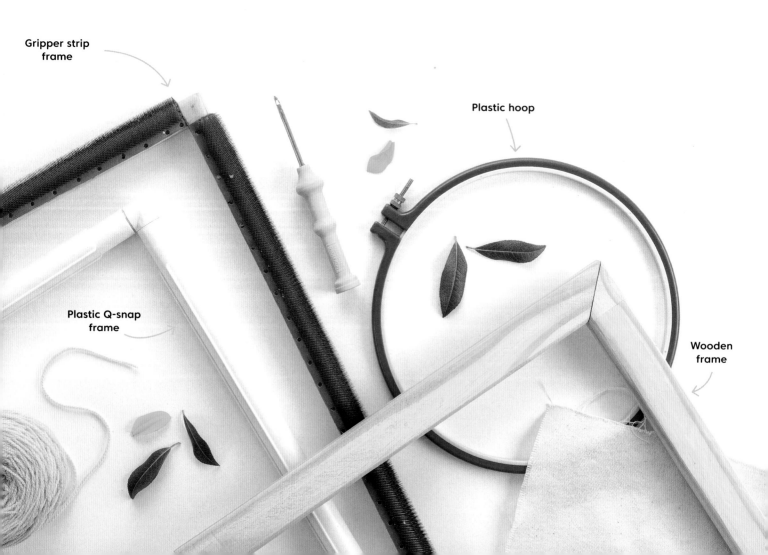

Gripper strip frame

Plastic hoop

Plastic Q-snap frame

Wooden frame

OTHER USEFUL EQUIPMENT

- Pins
- Latch-hook needle
- Tapestry or wool needle, with large eye and blunt point
- Light box
- Masking tape
- Permanent ink marker pens – thick and thin tips
- Embroidery marker pens (erasable with water or heat)
- Plastic eyes and noses, for amigurumi or felt dolls
- Pom-pom maker
- Lint or bobble remover
- Ruler or tape measure
- Metal bristle brush, for loop finishing
- Curved scissors, for creating tufting effect comfortably
- Fabric scissors
- Embroidery scissors and/or thread cutters

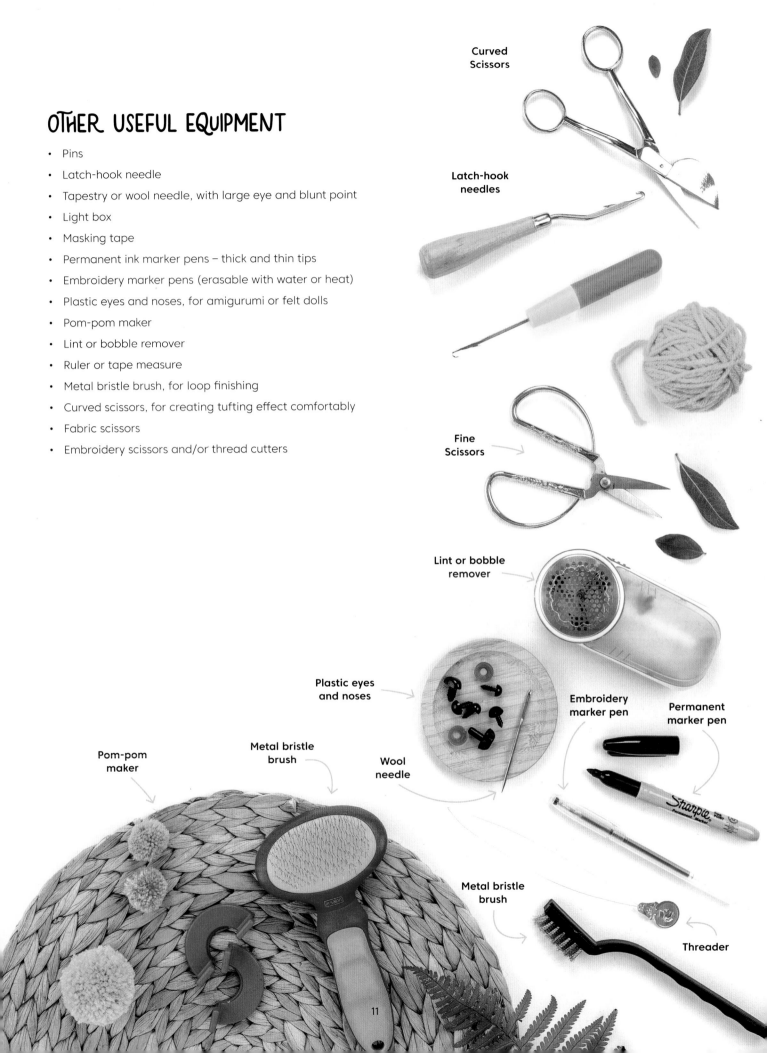

Curved Scissors

Latch-hook needles

Fine Scissors

Lint or bobble remover

Plastic eyes and noses

Embroidery marker pen

Permanent marker pen

Pom-pom maker

Metal bristle brush

Wool needle

Metal bristle brush

Threader

11

TRANSFERRING THE DESIGNS

I will now describe the method that works best for transferring the designs from paper to the fabric, plus give you some handy tips that help to make this process as easy and as accurate as possible.

It is advisable to protect the edges of your fabric from fraying before working on it. Either sew a line of straight or zigzag stitches along the edges using a sewing machine or overlocker (serger; **A)** or, even easier, wrap the edges with masking tape **(B)**.

I like to transfer designs to fabric by tracing. To do this, attach the design to the back of the fabric with masking tape. Turn the fabric over to the right side.

To be able to see the design clearly through the fabric to trace it, you need a light source. The best option is a light box, which designers, artists, animators and others use to look at transparencies, adjust designs and so on, as it has an even light across the entire surface **(C)**. Alternatively, try one of the following options:

- a glass table with a lamp or other light source underneath

- a window, sticking the fabric, with the design behind it, to the glass with masking tape

- a tablet or computer screen, tracing carefully directly from the screen.

To trace the lines of the design onto the right side of the fabric – apart from the final option – you will need a marker pen. My favourite ones for tracing have indelible black ink (so that the design doesn't rub off and is clearly visible). I use one with a thick tip for large projects and one with a fine tip for smaller projects or finer details. I only recommend this method for designs where the entire surface of the fabric will be covered with stitches, as otherwise the ink could be seen.

If, however, you want to embroider only some parts of the fabric or to use very light shades of yarn, it is best to use an embroidery marker pen instead. Some of these have ink that can be erased with water, others with heat. For the former, once you've finished the embroidery, simply rub the pen lines off with a piece of dampened cotton wool rather than submerge the entire piece in water. For ink erased with heat, use a hairdryer or iron to make the ink disappear.

When combining loops and flat stitches, the design must be drawn on both sides of the fabric. Using light-coloured fabric, transfer the design to the right side, as described, then turn the fabric over and trace it on the other side, following the lines showing through from the right side.

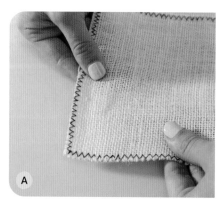

A

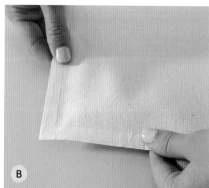

B

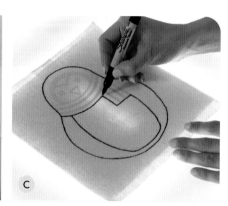

C

USING THE NEEDLE

Next, learn how to thread both slotted and slotless punch needles, plus the golden rules for using them properly for great results. Don't worry if you make a mistake – there are ways to fix them!

THREADING SLOTTED NEEDLES

1. Hold the needle with the slot facing up.

2. Without cutting the yarn off the ball, pass the yarn from the bottom to the top, through the metal ring at the base of the needle, if your needle has one **(A)**, then thread it through the eye at the tip, from the side of the slot outwards **(B)**.

3. Insert the rest of the yarn along the slot.

THREADING SLOTLESS NEEDLES

1. Pass the threader through the needle, entering from above and exiting through the bottom of the handle **(C)**.

2. Place the yarn in the loop of the threader that is sticking out of the handle **(D)**.

3. Pull the threader up **(E)**.

4. Take the tail of yarn and pass it through the side hole of the needle by hand or using the threader **(F)**.

Whatever type of needle you use, the tail of yarn that comes out of the eye should measure no more than 1 or 2cm (⅜ or ¾in).

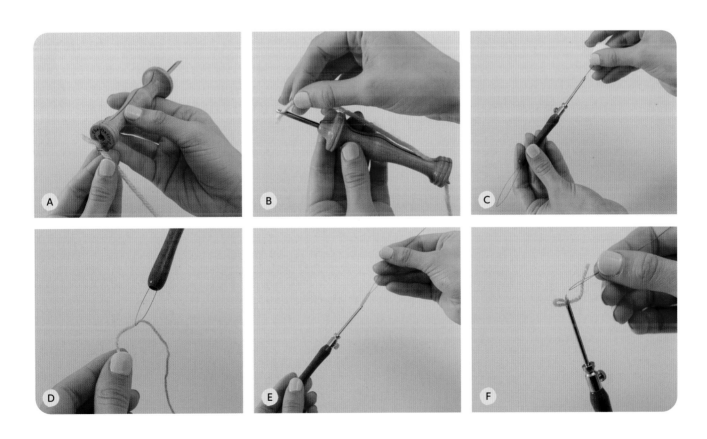

HOLDING THE NEEDLE

Hold it in the middle of the handle, as if it were a pen, with the slot or the bevelled part of the tip facing upwards.

> To help you to hold a slotless needle correctly, you can scratch and make a mark below the bevel on the handle with a permanent ink marker pen, so you know which way is up.

THE FOUR GOLDEN RULES

Not using the needle properly will cause the stitches to come loose. For best results, follow these golden rules.

RULE 1: Insert the point of the needle into a hole in the fabric, with the handle in line with the direction in which you want to stitch, then push until the handle touches the fabric. Never stop before it touches or the loops on the back will be different sizes and some might come out. See Finishing the Stitches for how to deal with the tail end.

RULE 2: To make the next stitch and not destroy the loop that you've just made, lift the needle gently and only a little above the surface of the fabric, then punch it into the fabric again, as in Rule 1. Repeat this movement in a line, following the design.

RULE 3: Rotate the needle as you progress over the area of the design you are working on so that the slot (or the bevelled part of the point if you have a slotless needle) always faces where you are about to stitch.

RULE 4: The yarn should slide easily inside the needle. To enable this to happen, unwind lengths of yarn from the ball as it is consumed, to avoid pulling. Check that the yarn is not held down by anything and that there are no knots in the ball, as then the stitch will be pulled out of the fabric.

FIXING MISTAKES

Simply raise the needle and undo the stitch or stitches concerned. Hold the stitches you want to keep with one finger as you do this, so that they do not come loose **(G)**. Rub the weft of the fabric with the point of the needle or fine-tipped scissors to close the holes made and make the fabric smooth.

Before continuing, carefully pull the yarn back through the needle. There should be no excess yarn between the point of the needle and the fabric.

If the yarn runs out, thread the needle and punch it into the last hole used, so that there are two yarn tails in the same hole on the back.

FINISHING THE STITCHES

There are two options.

- **Cut the yarn from the front:** Holding the last stitch with your finger to stop it coming loose, gently lift the needle. Cut the yarn, leaving 1 or 2 cm (⅜ or ¾in), and bring that tail back with the help of scissors or the tip of the needle **(H)**.

- **Cut the yarn directly on the back:** If you are using a slotless needle, make the last stitch and, without removing the needle, turn the hoop or frame over. Pull a little yarn out from the side eye of the needle and cut. If the needle is slotted, however, never pull the yarn from the slot, because when you withdraw the needle, the yarn will go to the other side **(I)**.

Use either on of these options for the tail end of the initial stitch.

Always pass tails to the side with the loops, whether you are doing flat or loopy stitches. Next to loops, cut tails to the same height, so that they blend in. In areas of flat stitches, pass tails back to the other side to hide them, giving a clean finish. Never leave a tail on the flat side, because it is the most fragile side. If caught, it could loosen the rest of the stitches.

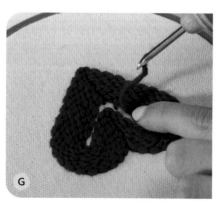

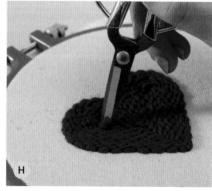

TRADITIONAL PUNCH NEEDLE STITCHES

The most fundamental and oldest stitches made using the punch needle technique are flat stitches and loops. The difference is simply whether you embroider from the front or from the back.

Whether you use flat or loopy stitches, you will always embroider in a brick pattern – that is, in each new row, stagger every stitch by half a stitch in relation to those in the row below **(A)**. So, in a second row of stitches, punch the needle into the fabric at the point that is over the middle of the stitch below it. This pattern serves the same purpose as it does in a brick wall: it achieves a stronger structure. Also, it is guaranteed to fully cover the fabric.

FLAT STITCH

Flat stitches **(B)** are embroidered from the front of the fabric, so you can simply transfer your chosen design to the fabric the right way round, not as a mirror image of it. With these stitches, you have to be careful because what you are embroidering is the final finish (unlike the loops). We could say that it is an 'accuser' of a stitch, as any imperfections will be seen, so you have to embroider carefully and evenly.

LOOPS

Loops **(C)** are embroidered from the back of the fabric, so you will need to transfer the design onto the back of the fabric so that it is a mirror image of what is on the front (simply follow the steps described in Transferring the Designs to do this). Don't forget, especially when embroidering letters or numbers, or everything will be in reverse!

You can make the loops different heights to create texture. To do this, use needles of different lengths, adjustable needles or (a cheaper alternative) add one or more 'stops' to your needle to make your loops shorter.

The shorter the loop, the closer together you need to place your stitches. The longer your loop, therefore, the further apart you can make the stitches, as the volume taken up by the bigger loops of yarn means that they will still cover the fabric.

The objective is to cover the entire surface of the fabric using the right and necessary numbers of stitches.

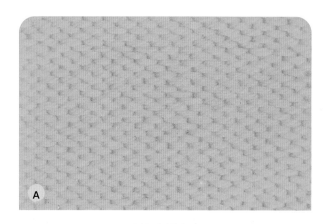

A

B

C

SPECIAL TREATMENTS & FINISHES

By finishing the loops in the ways described here, they can be given quite different textures and looks, adding extra dimension to your punch needle projects and making them wonderfully tactile.

Tufting

This involves cutting previously embroidered loops through at the tip, so that each loop becomes two strands **(A)**. Loops of any height can be cut, except for extremely short ones. The resulting effect is similar to the fur of a soft toy or stuffed animal **(B)**. For most yarns, the insides of the strands look darker than the outsides, so when you cut the loops the darker yarn interior will be seen. Don't forget this when choosing your yarn, to avoid surprises when the colour changes. It is advisable to glue the back.

Brushing

After embroidering a surface with loops, you can brush them to create a furry effect **(C)**. It is best to use metal bristle brushes because they are the strongest. The loops can be brushed several times in different directions to ensure an even finish **(D)**. To tidy up the final result, you can trim the bits that are too long. This treatment only works with wool or acrylic yarns, not other fibres, such as cotton and silk.

Pom-pom

Did you know that you can also carve your embroidery?

1. Form loop stitches that are as tall and close together as possible. The aim is that the loops are very densely clustered together **(E, F)**.

2. Then comes the funniest (and messiest) moment! Use sharp scissors to cut the loops **(G)** and trim to carve your shape. It is best to cut little by little so that you don't cut too much and spoil the shape.

3. From time to time remove the fluff or lint by hand, or vacuum it off at the lowest suction level so as not to damage the embroidery. The result of this effect is similar to a pom-pom **(H)**. As with tufting, bear in mind the colour it will be once it has been cut. It is advisable to glue the back.

MODERN PUNCH NEEDLE STITCHES

Modern stitches aren't used to cover surfaces, they are used for decoration. They tend to be more fragile than traditional filling stitches, so they need to be secured on the back, by making knots or with glue. Some modern stitches are worked from the front of the fabric, others from the back. To finish the stitches, cut the yarn on the front or directly on the back as described under Finishing the stitches.

FROM THE BACK OF THE FABRIC

XL loops

Of course, you can make XL loops with a long needle, but if you don't have one or you want to make a much longer loop than the needle you are using allows, you can simply use your other hand.

1. Looking at the back of your embroidery, form a traditional loop, but keep the needle in the hole.

2. With your other hand, hold the loop you have made and lengthen it **(A)**.

3. You can also embroider looking at the front, with the needle under the fabric **(B)**, so you can see the result and check the size of the loops **(C)**. Remember, this stitch is decorative, for accent details (such as flowers), not larger areas; XL loops are never exactly the same height, so the variations would be very evident.

Stem stitch

The most difficult thing to embroider with loops is outlines. Using stem stitch instead creates a solid, tubular line, which is much more effective **(D)**.

1. Change the position of your needle so, instead of the slot or the bevelled tip facing the direction in which the stitches are to go, turn the needle 90 degrees to the left **(E)**.

2. Embroider the stitches as close together as possible.

Thin chain stitch

1. Looking at the front of your embroidery, form a traditional loop, but with the needle under your hoop or embroidery frame **(F)**. Remember that the slot or the bevelled tip of the needle should point in the direction in which the stitches are to go.

2. Before making the next stitch, hold the loop down with your other hand **(G)**.

3. Insert the needle, again from below, coming up in the middle of the first loop, to form the second loop in the chain **(H)**. Gently pull the yarn in the needle up so that the chain sits snugly against the fabric.

4. Repeat these four steps – make a loop, lay it down, come up inside the loop to form the next loop and gently pull the yarn in the needle up **(I)** – until the chain stitching is the right length and shape.

5. Each time you pull the yarn in the needle up so that the chain sits snugly against the fabric, the loop in the needle grows. When it becomes annoyingly long, pull the yarn below the fabric to make it smaller again **(J)**.

6. To finish, make a loop inside the final one and cut the yarn, leaving a tail of about 2cm (¾in; **K**).

7. With a latch-hook or crochet hook, come up just beyond the final loop, hook the tail **(L)** and pull it down to the back of your work. In this way, the loop will be held in place on the front and you can tie the end pulled through in a knot with the other tails on the back.

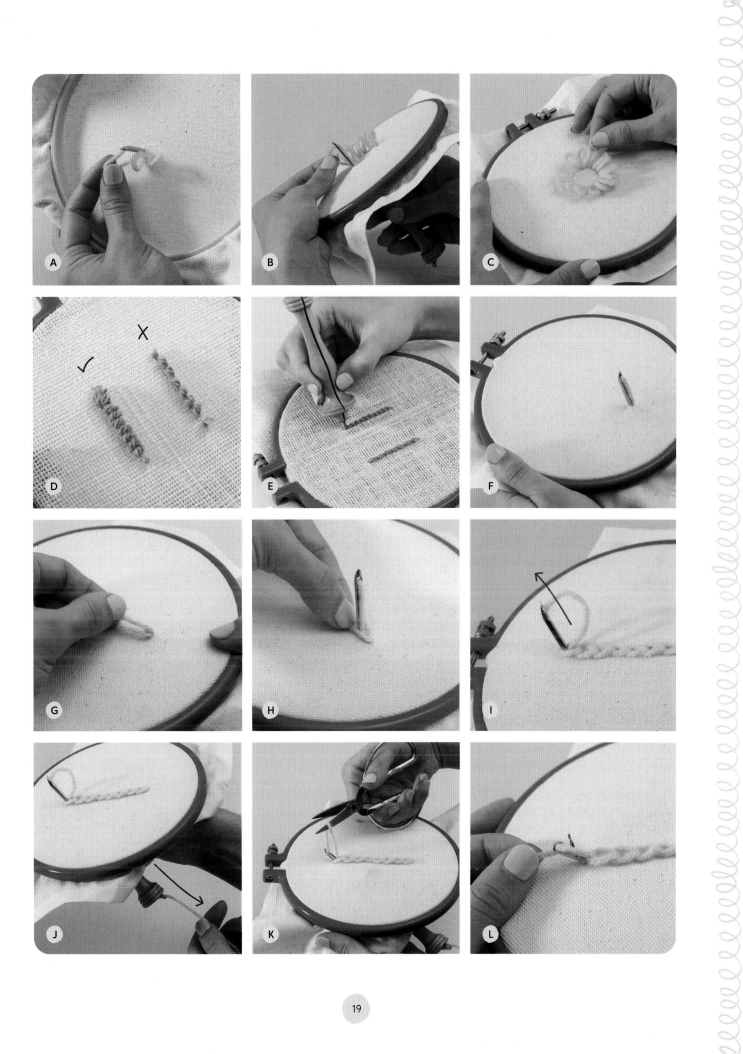

FROM THE FRONT OF THE FABRIC

Thick chain stitch

1. Looking at the front of your embroidery, form a loop by punching the needle into the fabric, then lifting the needle and holding the yarn with your finger. Push the needle back into the original hole to complete **(M)**.

2. Insert the tip of the needle into the loop **(N)**, lean it forwards so that the loop lies down on the fabric, being careful not to pull it, then push the needle into the fabric **(O)**. Make a second loop in this hole in the same way as the first.

3. Repeat the steps again, as required.

4. To finish, after stretching the final loop and punching into it, make a short flat stitch over the tip of the loop to hold it in place **(P)**.

Spike or arrow stitch

1. Start by embroidering a 'V' in flat stitches from right to left.

2. Close the 'V', forming a triangle, but slope this stitch slightly upwards, pushing the tip of the needle in just above the first hole, top right of the 'V' **(Q)**.

3. Repeat, sitting the inverted triangles inside one another **(R)**, to form a wheat ear or herringbone pattern.

4. This stitch can be used to embroider decorative bands. To finish, cut the yarn **(S)** and poke the tail back through the hole it is sticking out of or cut directly on the back.

5. When embroidering a wheat ear or similar, instead of completing the final triangle, make a 'V' **(T)** and embroider a stem using a line of traditional flat stitches **(U)**.

Fill stitch stripes

It is best to use open-weave fabrics, so that the holes are visible. It is also helpful to have good light and even a magnifying glass, to help you count the holes in the fabric.

1. Work a line of traditional flat stitches, all the same length, the same number of holes in the fabric covered by each **(V)**. I punched the needle every five holes.

2. Work the next line of flat stitches close to the first, each stitch the same length as those in the first line **(W)**. Keep repeating the lines of stitches, close together.

3. It is no longer necessary to count the holes. Simply insert the needle at the same point as was punched in the previous row.

4. As you continue, a striped effect will be generated **(X)**.

To be able to see the holes in the fabric clearly to count them, place a light source underneath your work (a lamp, torch, light box or your phone).

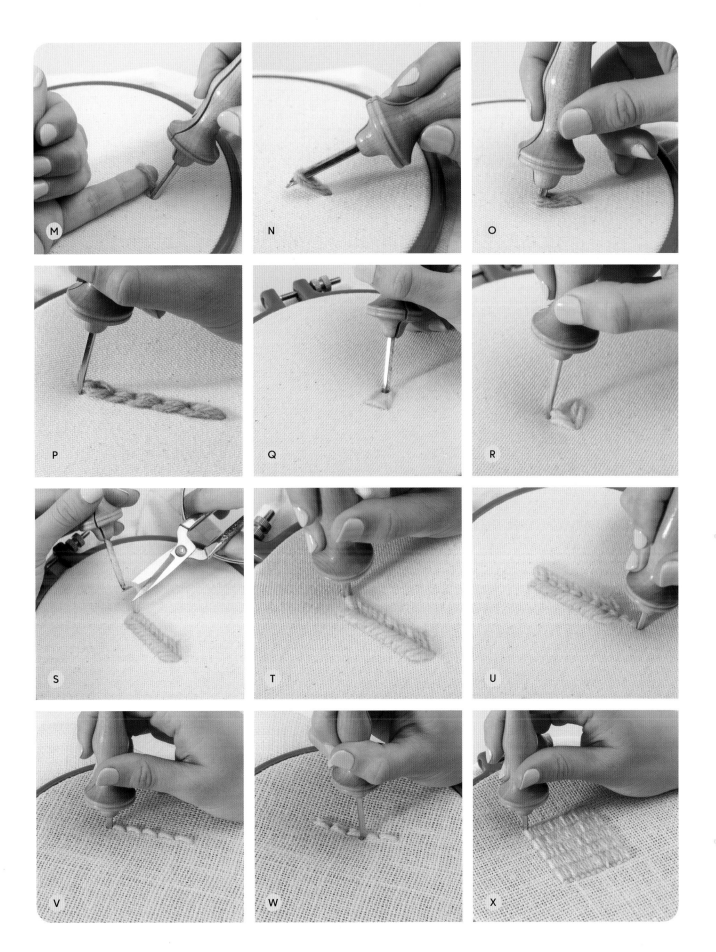

Satin stitch

This stitch is easy and useful for filling shapes with a smooth texture.

1. Draw the shape to be filled on your fabric.

2. Punch the needle from one side of the shape to the other **(Y)**, then lay stitches next to one another, following the shape along the top and bottom.

3. For a long stitch, hold it down as you push the needle in on the far side **(Z)** so that it is not too tight and to ensure that you don't pull it loose in the process of making it. The longer the stitch, the more fragile it will be. (See Fringe if you want to secure the stitches.)

Rose stitch

For this stitch, long stitches are made in a spiral, from the centre out, to make the layers of petals.

1. Make a tiny triangle with a few flat stitches **(AA)** to form the centre of the rose.

2. Make longer stitches round the centre **(BB)**, inserting the needle at the centre of each side, close to and overlapping previous stitches.

3. Continue making longer stitches in a spiral and inserting the needle at the centre of each of the now longer sides. Ensure that the long stitches overlap the bud formed in the centre, so that the rose grows in height as well as diameter **(CC)**.

4. Once the rose is the desired size, embroider an outline with shorter flat stitches to support it **(DD)**.

Leaf stitch

1. Draw a leaf on your fabric.

2. From the tip towards the centre of the leaf, to the first vein, work a flat stitch **(EE)**.

3. Focusing only on the left or right half of the leaf, form a long stitch from the central midline to the edge **(FF)**.

4. Return from the edge to the midline diagonally **(GG)**, to mimic the texture of leaves, using another long stitch and placing it close enough to the first to cover the fabric. Contrary to the usual way of working, the slot or the bevelled tip of the needle does not face the direction in which the stitches are being formed but, instead, you need to move the needle sideways. Continue making stitches down the length of the half of the leaf you are working on.

5. If the stitches are long, hold them with your finger as you are forming them **(HH)**, as described for Satin stitch, so that they don't become too tight or come loose.

6. When you reach the bottom of the leaf, don't cut the yarn but continue embroidering up the other half **(II)**. Remember to keep the stitches diagonal, sloping them the other way, like the veins on a leaf.

7. When you reach the tip again, you can end the leaf there or embroider a line of flat stitches down the centre and to form a stem **(JJ)**. These stitches will improve the finish, as they cover any imperfections where the long stitches meet in the middle of the leaf.

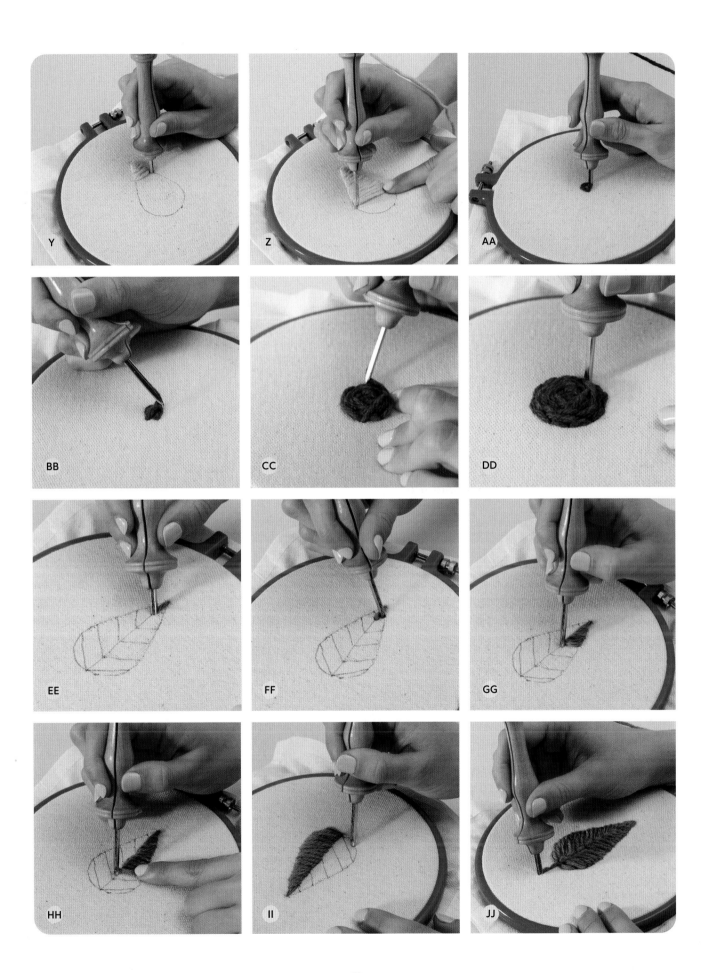

Cross stitch line

1. Embroider a line using flat stitches **(KK)**.

2. Once the line is finished, go back to the beginning, making diagonal stitches across the line at even intervals and all the same length **(LL)**.

3. An option then is to work opposite diagonal stitches across the previous diagonal stitches, to form crosses and make the line thicker **(MM)**.

Wrapped cord

This uses satin stitch, but an external element is added: a thick cord. You can use any braided cord, such as macramé or nylon cord. The aim is to use the cord as a filler to achieve very three-dimensional lines and shapes.

1. Place the cord in the desired shape on your fabric. You can use pins to hold it in place **(NN)**. It is not necessary to assemble the entire shape, it can be done little by little to make it easier.

2. Cover the cord with satin stitches (long stitches), going from one side to the other, placing each stitch close to the next one **(OO)** to cover the cord completely.

3. To finish, trim the cord and work some flat stitches round the ends to cover them. Start with stitches the width of the cord, then decrease the size until everything is covered **(PP)**.

Fringe

1. Form long stitches, from bottom to top, all the same length **(QQ)**. How long they are will depend on the length the fringe needs to be. It is best to make them a little longer than desired and trim any excess later.

2. Hold the yarn with your finger while forming the long stitches **(RR)**, so that they don't pull and come loose.

3. Place the rows close together so that the fringing will be dense.

4. You can then punch a line of flat stitches along the top of the fringe **(SS)** to secure it.

5. To finish, simply cut the yarn so that it is the same length as the rest of the fringe.

6. On the back, pass a wool needle threaded with a piece of yarn through the centre of the loops along the top of the fringe **(TT)**. Take care not to miss any, then tie a thick knot so that it does not go through the loops. This will strengthen the stitches as they are usually prone to coming loose.

7. On the front, lift the loops out of the fabric along the bottom edge of the fringe **(UU)** and cut the tip of each loop.

8. Trim the fringe, as though you were a hairdresser, so the bottom edge is straight **(VV)**.

I prefer using cotton, fine wool or acrylic yarn to make fringes on small pieces. Thick yarns are recommended for very large projects, as the weight will help them to hang well. Also, you can comb them to separate the strands and make them look fuller.

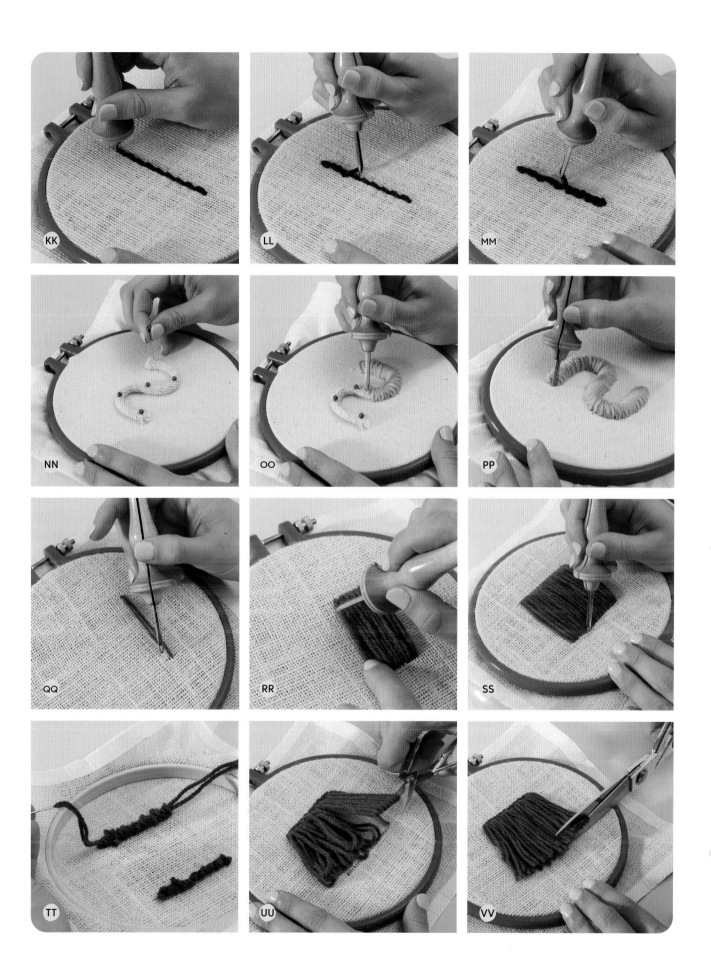

YOUR EMBROIDERY STRATEGY

By analysing your design, you can create your 'embroidery strategy', planning where to start and next steps. These examples will help you.

Combining flat and loopy stitches

It is best to start with the loops, leaving areas to be filled with flat stitches to the end **(A)**. If you do it the other way round, you won't be able to see the flat-stitched areas fully when forming the loops, so you may accidentally push some stitches, spoiling the work. When embroidering flat stitches next to areas with loops, hold the loops away with your other hand, so you can cover all the fabric with stitches.

Special treatments and finishes for loops

It is easiest to do a brushed finish or carving for a pom-pom first **(B)**. Why? Because trying to brush only part of a finished embroidery with force with a wire brush without touching adjoining areas is impossible, so only the centre will have the brushed finish you want and the edges will not. Similarly, it is hard to form a pom-pom when it is surrounded by other stitches, then annoying for your work to be covered with fluff!

Fine lines for areas of flat stitch

It is always a good idea to embroider fine lines first. When creating outlines and other fine lines, there is a risk that the background stitches will partially cover them, so they will be less visible. For the giraffe's shirt front, for example **(C)**, begin by embroidering the black vertical lines first, as they are the finest details, then the white background. Having embroidered the background, however, the black lines will be somewhat submerged. Simply embroider them again, punching the needle in the same holes as before. That way, the lines will be a little plumper, so they will stand out.

All the above

Brushing should always be done first, then any areas of pom-pom or loops, followed by flat stitch fine lines, then areas of flat stitch and, finally, redoing flat stitch fine lines.

SEWING & FILLING

To bring your completed flat pieces of punch needle embroidery to life by making them three-dimensional, you need to do some sewing, then filling, in one of two ways.

Single-sided toy, using a sewing machine

With this method, the back of the toy will not be embroidered. You can choose any type of fabric.

1. Place the embroidery right side down on the right side of the fabric for the back and pin the layers together.

2. Trim off the excess fabric (both layers), following the outline of the embroidery, leaving a 3cm (1⅛in) seam allowance all the way round **(A)**.

3. If you have embroidered the ears separately (see Making the Toys), place them right side down between the layers on each side of the head, with the tab on the wider edges of the ears placed so that the edge of the embroidery lies along the seamline (3cm/1⅛in in from the edge) and the tips point towards the centre of the toy. Pin in place **(B)**.

4. Sew along the seamline (3cm/1⅛in in from the edge around the outside of the shape) with a sewing machine, leaving an opening of about 5 cm (2in) along one leg, between paw and neck. This is so that you can turn the toy out and insert the filling **(C)**.

5. Gently turn the toy right side out through the opening **(D)**.

6. Stuff. Use a long rod, such as a thick knitting needle, to push the filling into the legs and paws **(E)**.

7. Tuck in the seam allowances along the 5cm (2in) opening and sew closed with whip or invisible stitches **(F)**.

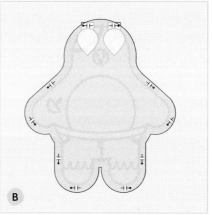

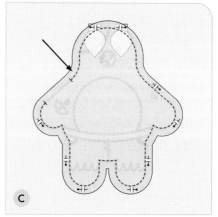

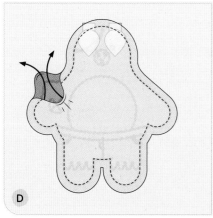

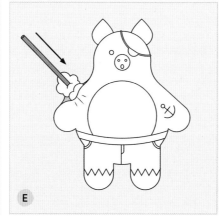

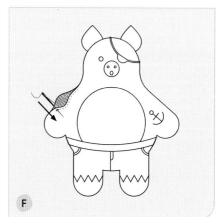

Double-sided toy, using whip stitches

Use this method if you have also embroidered the back of your toy. It takes more time, but is perfect if you either don't have or don't like using a sewing machine. An advantage of embroidering the back is that the toy looks more 3D and it's easier to cover any little mistakes around the edges.

1. Draw a line on the fabric around the front and back pieces that is 3cm (1⅛in) away from the edge of your embroidery. This margin is the seam allowance **(G)**.

2. Cover the lines you have drawn with glue **(H)**. The glue will prevent the fabric from fraying.

3. Once the glue is dry, cut the front and back pieces out along the lines **(I)**.

4. With wrong sides together, lay the front on the back, matching up the design along the edges, and pin **(J)**.

5. Thread a wool or darning needle (with a large eye and blunt or sharp point) with a piece of matching yarn about the length of your arm. No knot is needed.

6. Turn the seam allowances of both layers to the inside. Insert the needle through the folded edge of the side nearest you as close as possible to the edge of the embroidery, so that no fabric is visible, and then take it through the very edge of the folded edge of the other side **(K)**.

7. Pull the yarn through until there is a small tail (about 3 cm/1⅛in). Tuck it inside the toy and to one side **(L, M)**.

8. Bringing the yarn up and over the seam, insert the needle through the side nearest you again, close to the first stitch, and take it back through the other side, close to the first stitch **(M)**. The stitch across the seam is your first whip stitch.

9. Repeat this process until the colour of the embroidery each side of the seam changes or the yarn runs out. In either case, to finish, insert the needle through the whip stitches towards the first stitch and come out as far back as possible. Cut the yarn flush **(N)**.

10. If you have embroidered the ears separately (see Making the Toys), insert them into the seam, right side (flat stitches) facing to the front (loops at the back) and tabs inside, so that only embroidery can be seen along the seam. Pin in place **(O)**. It is easiest to sew each one in after you have whip stitched the part of the seam up to the right-hand edge of an ear. For each ear, continue using the yarn in your needle but work some running stitches the full width of each ear to secure them, passing the needle through the three layers of fabric (the front, ear tab and back) **(P)**.

11. Whip stitch the rest of the seam, leaving about 5 cm (2in) open for filling. Use a long rod, such as a thick knitting needle, to push the filling into the legs and paws **(Q)**.

12. Sew the hole closed with whip stitch **(R)**.

Commonly polyester or acrylic stuffing is used, but alternatives are bean bag filling, beads, seeds, sponge, leftover fabric and yarn.

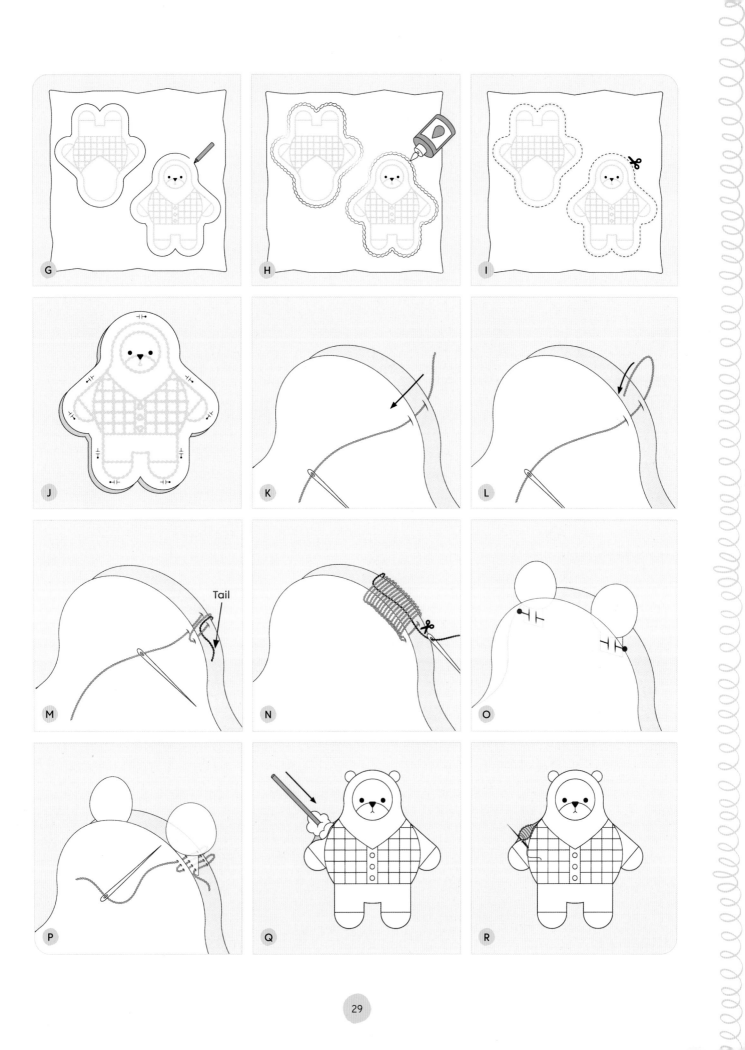

MAKING THE TOYS

I will tell you the stories of 20 cute characters as I explain how to turn them into toys. In this way you can enjoy them and apply everything you learn in this book. Don't be afraid of the needle – let's get started!

For most of the toys I used two needles of different thicknesses, to achieve a variety of textures, and the corresponding thickness of yarn for each one. I used panama fabric, but you can use any fabric that has 5 or 6 holes per cm (⅜in).

> Remember that the colours, yarns, thicknesses and designs given are just suggestions. The more creative you are with your choices, the better!

For each toy I have provided actual-size templates, plus an illustration that shows which stitches are used where and in what order in the design. Most of the designs are symmetrical, but for asymmetrical designs the whole pattern has been provided, to be copied as described in step 2. If the design is symmetrical, only half the pattern has been provided, so it needs to be mirrored to give you the whole pattern. How to do this is also described in step 2.

Follow these steps to make all the toys.

1. Choose a piece of fabric that is large enough to fit the front or front and back templates of the toy you want to make, plus enough of a margin around it or them to overhang the frame or hoop of your choice (around 5 to 10cm/2 to 4in) larger all round than your design).

2. Trace the outline for the right or top half of the design for the front of the toy onto a sheet of paper with a black marker pen to create a template. Then fold the sheet of paper in half and trace along the lines you drew to create the other half of the template. A light source below the paper can help with this (see Transferring the Designs). Open to see the front of your toy. If you are embroidering the back, repeat to create a template for the left or lower half of the design, which is the back. Follow any instructions to add any non-symmetrical parts to your templates.

3. At this point you can choose to keep or change your toy's outfit. For example, you can replace the lion's shirt with the sloth's sweater. As all the animals are the same shape, it's easy to swap their clothing. Trace your chosen clothing onto your front and back templates.

4. Stick your paper template to the back of your fabric with masking tape. Transfer the design to the fabric by tracing it on the front **(A)**. Almost all the toys have a combination of flat and loopy stitches, so if yours does, the design must be transferred to both sides of the fabric. As before, see Transferring the Designs for tips on how to do this. Again, repeat if you are embroidering the back.

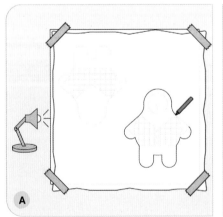

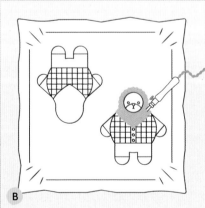

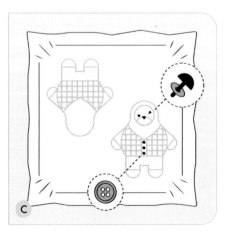

5. Stretch the fabric on your embroidery hoop or frame.

6. If you are being creative, revisit Your Embroidery Strategy to plan the order for your stitches. If you are following the details given for each toy, however, simply work the stitches in the order indicated by the numbers in the text and illustration. Ready? Let's punch **(B)**!

7. Once finished, attach any necessary accessories, such as eyes, noses, buttons, pom-poms ... whatever you want to make your toy unique **(C)**.

8. There are three ways in which the ears are made, depending on what suits the design best.

Pom-poms added: the best option for rounded ears, such as Berta Bear or Karim Koala. Make pom-poms of the desired size, leaving the tails of yarn used to tie them at the centre long. For each ear, thread a wool needle with both tails, pierce the fabric on the right side and knot the tails together on the inside **(D)**.

Embroidered separately: for floppy ears, such as Enrique Elephant or Susana Sheep, trace both ears onto your fabric (making one the mirror image of the other), including tabs. Embroider them with flat stitches on the right sides, loops on the back, and form the stitches carefully so that they all look nice, as both sides will be seen **(E)**. Finish with a thick line of glue around the outside edge of the whole ear, as close to the embroidery as possible **(F)**. Once the glue has dried, trim the ears along the glued lines to neaten, leaving the tabs on **(G)**. The tabs are needed to attach the ears to the toy.

Included: ears that are flat and rounded are simply included in the outline of the toy and so are embroidered along with the rest of the character's body. These kinds of ears can be found on Felipe Fox and Mateo Monkey.

9. If you are making a double-sided toy, embroider the back next.

10. Weave in and finish any tail ends (see Using the Needle: Finishing the Stitches), then you can glue the back, but only if necessary to secure your stitches **(H)**.

11. Sew the parts of your toy together and fill with stuffing to finish (see Sewing & Filling).

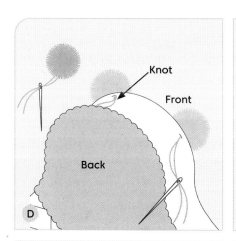

Knot

Front

Back

D

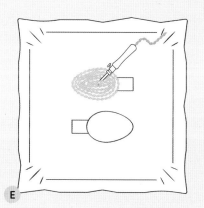

E

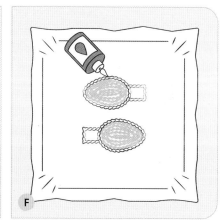

F

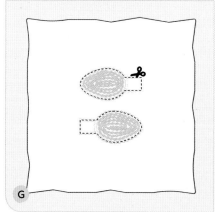

G

Back

H

As with all handmade items, treat your toys carefully to ensure they last. Despite it being tempting to give them to little ones, I recommend that they be used for decoration, not played with. To keep the toys in good condition, avoid washing and display them out of direct sunlight. Shake them once a week, vacuuming them (on the lowest setting) from time to time to prevent dust build-up.

BERTA BEAR

Berta needs to learn to swim, but she is a very lazy bear. Although she doesn't like to exercise, she also doesn't like to admit that she can't swim! She is thinking that maybe she will go to the pool very early in the morning or at night so no one will see her trying. They are all excuses, though. She has now bought the cutest swimsuit in the shop so she will feel compelled to sign up for swimming classes, but she hasn't yet. Instead, she likes to look in the mirror with her swimsuit on and that is enough for her for now.

MATERIALS

- Medium punch needle (3mm diameter), 3cm/1⅛in length, for the body, face, swimsuit, flowers and leaves.
- Medium long punch needle (3mm diameter), 6cm/2⅜in length or work XL loops, for the flounce.
- Adjustable fine punch needle (2mm diameter), 4cm/1⅝in length, for the snout and final contours.
- Panama fabric or similar, with 5 holes per cm (⅜in).
- Aran (US 4 medium, worsted) yarn: dark brown for the body, ears, tail and one of the flowers; light brown for the face; pink and purple for the swimsuit; green for the leaves; white for the flounce and one of the flowers.
- 4 ply, baby (US 2 fine, fingering) yarn: white for the snout.
- Golden embroidery silk or shiny yarn: for the final contours of the leaves, flowers, waist and crossed straps.
- Plastic eyes and nose.

EMBROIDERY

FRONT
1. Snout: pom-pom.
2. Body: tufting.
3. Waist: cross stitch line.
4. Flounce: XL loops (worked through the holes of the cross stitches).
5. Flowers: rose stitch.
6. Leaves: leaf stitch.
7. Face: flat stitch.
8. Swimsuit: flat stitch.
9. Contours: flat stitch.

BACK
10. Body: tufting.
11. Waist: cross stitch line.
12. Flounce: XL loops (worked through the holes of the cross stitches).
13. Crossed straps: thick chain stitch.
14. Swimsuit: flat stitch.
15. Contours: Flat stitch

EXTRAS
- Make pom-poms for ears and tail.

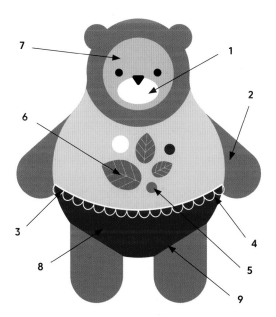

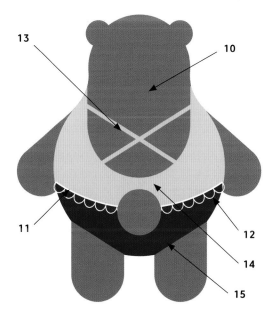

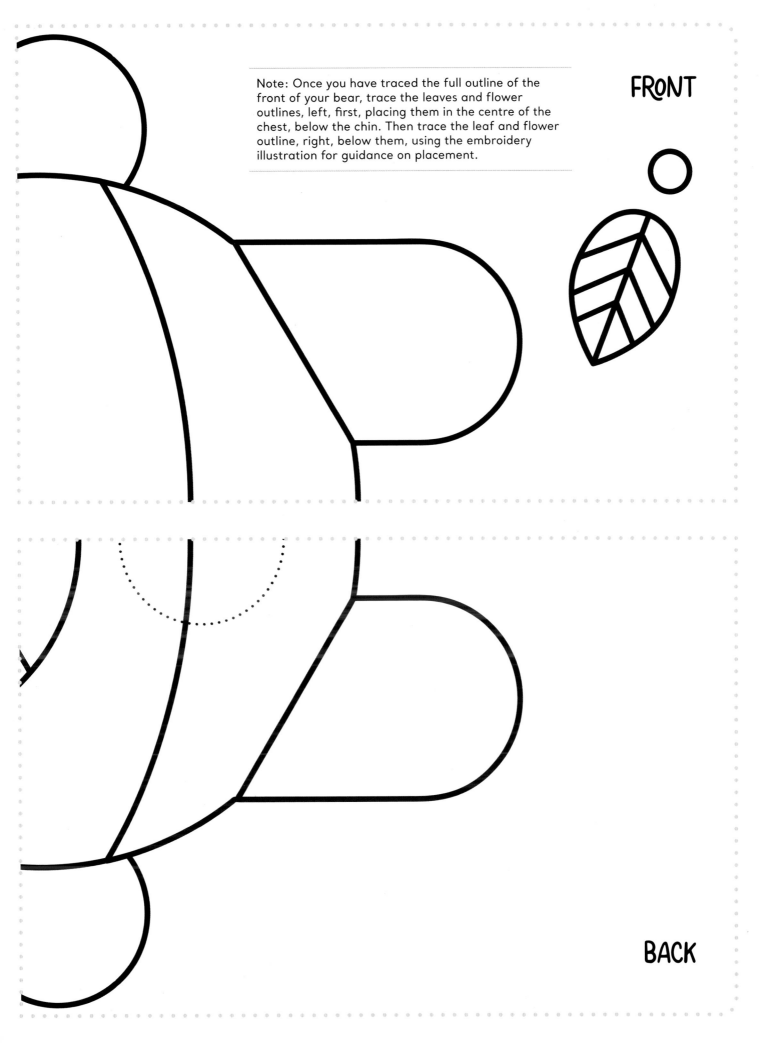

Note: Once you have traced the full outline of the front of your bear, trace the leaves and flower outlines, left, first, placing them in the centre of the chest, below the chin. Then trace the leaf and flower outline, right, below them, using the embroidery illustration for guidance on placement.

FRONT

BACK

BRUNO BEAVER

Bruno could be a union leader or a lawyer or simply dedicate himself to participating in debates of all kinds. The truth is, he really likes to fight and argue – and win! Don't be fooled by his uniform, he is not a soldier. He wears his grandfather's military helmet, like a 'method' actor, to get into character as a warrior who will not give up.

MATERIALS

- Medium punch needle (3mm diameter), 3cm/1⅛in length, for helmet, face, body, paws, teeth and belt.
- Medium long punch needle (3mm diameter), 6cm/2⅜in length or work XL loops, for the snout, wooden pouch and tail.
- Adjustable fine punch needle (2mm diameter), 4cm/1⅝in length, for the centreline of the front teeth and chest contour.
- Panama fabric or similar, with 5 holes per cm (⅜in).
- Aran (US 4 medium, worsted) yarn: beige for snout, chest, helmet and wooden pouch lines; black for belt, helmet and paws; two shades of brown: one for the fur and ears, and other for the wooden pouch and helmet; green for the helmet; white for the teeth.
- 4 ply, baby (US 2 fine, fingering) yarn: black for the centreline of the teeth.
- Golden embroidery silk or shiny yarn: for the final contours of the chest.
- Plastic eyes and nose.

EMBROIDERY

FRONT

1. Snout: pom-pom.
2. Wooden pouch: pom-pom.
3. Helmet: loops.
4. Chest: flat stitch.
5. Face and body: flat stitch.
6. Teeth: flat stitch.
7. Centreline of teeth: flat stitch.
8. Belt: flat stitch.
9. Paws: flat stitch.
10. Chest contour: flat stitch.

BACK

11. Tail: pom-pom.
12. Helmet: loops.
13. Body: flat stitch.
14. Belt: flat stitch.
15. Paws: flat stitch.

EXTRAS

- Make pom-poms for ears.

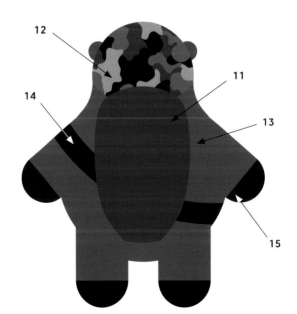

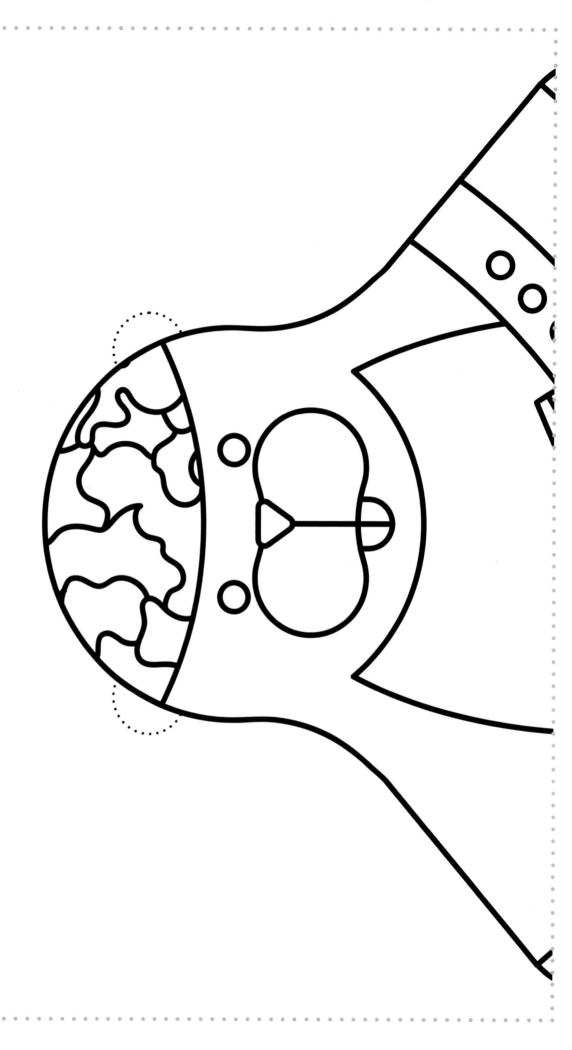

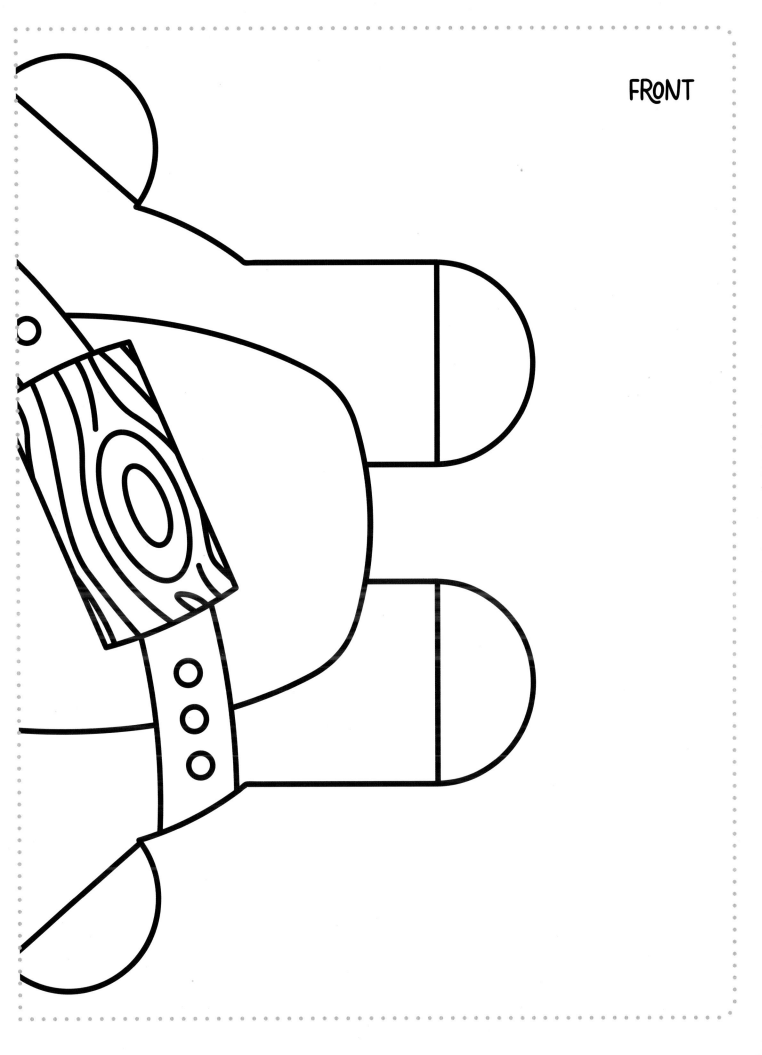

FRONT

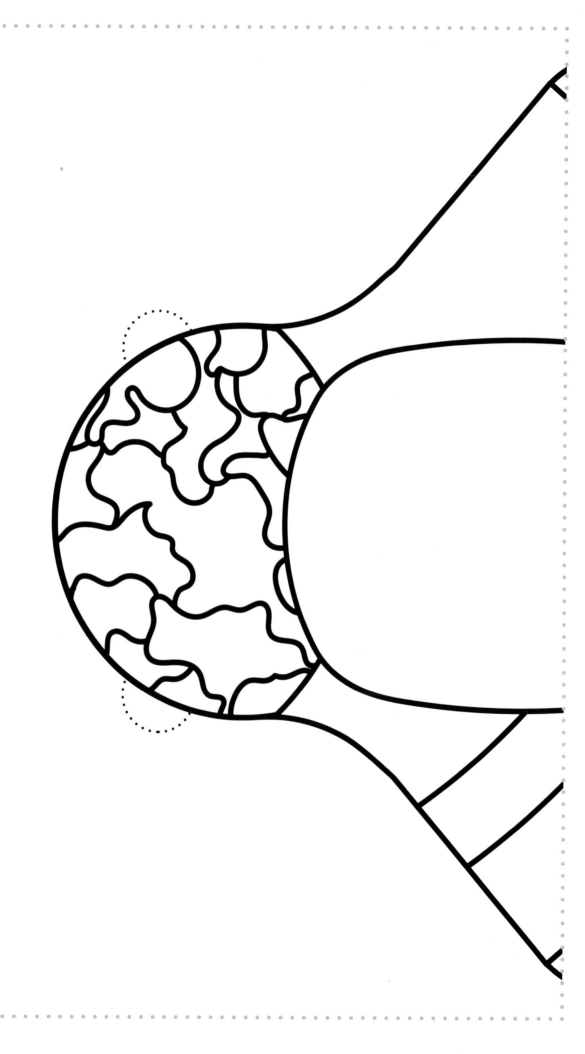

BACK

CAMILO CROCODILE

Camilo is a freelance software engineer, who works from home. He has a fully equipped desk next to the kitchen, with two curved monitors, a keyboard with lights, an ergonomic mouse and headphones with a microphone. He doesn't have a dress code for work. In fact, he hardly wears any clothes when he's working – he spends all day in his boxer shorts! Camilo can go to the shops or gym at times that would be outrageous for office workers. He can be seen at 11 in the morning exercising in the park or at 3 in the afternoon buying a gift. 'What does that guy do?' people think as they pass him. Well, Camilo is a freelance software engineer who works in his underwear.

MATERIALS

- Medium punch needle (3mm diameter), 4cm/1⅝in length, for the head, body, chest and legs.
- Medium long punch needle (3mm diameter), 6cm/2⅜in length or work XL loops, for the scales, snout and back lines, using stops to make the loops a little shorter.
- Adjustable fine punch needle (2mm diameter), 2.5cm/1in length, for the fangs and boxer shorts.
- Panama fabric or similar, with 5 holes per cm (⅜in).
- Aran (US 4 medium, worsted) yarn: dark green for head, body and paws; light green for body lines; yellow for chest and scales.
- 4 ply, baby (US 2 fine, fingering) yarn: white for boxer shorts and fangs; red for hearts on boxer shorts.
- Golden embroidery silk or shiny yarn: for the final contours of the chest.
- Plastic eyes and tiny eyes for nostrils.

EMBROIDERY

FRONT

1. Snout lines: stem stitch.
2. Head: loops.
3. Fangs: flat stitch.
4. Chest: fill stitch stripes.
5. Legs: flat stitch.
6. Boxer shorts: flat stitch.
7. Hearts on boxer shorts: flat stitch.

BACK

8. Scales: tufted XL loops.
9. Back lines: flat stitch.
10. Back and legs: flat stitch.
11. Boxer shorts: flat stitch.
12. Hearts on boxer shorts: flat stitch.
13. Back lines: if necessary, redo with flat stitch.

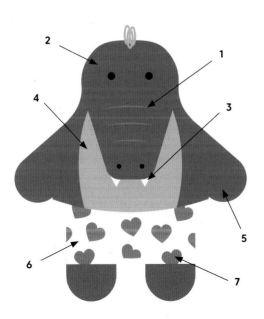
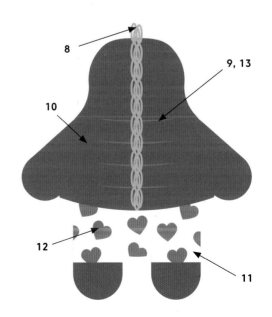

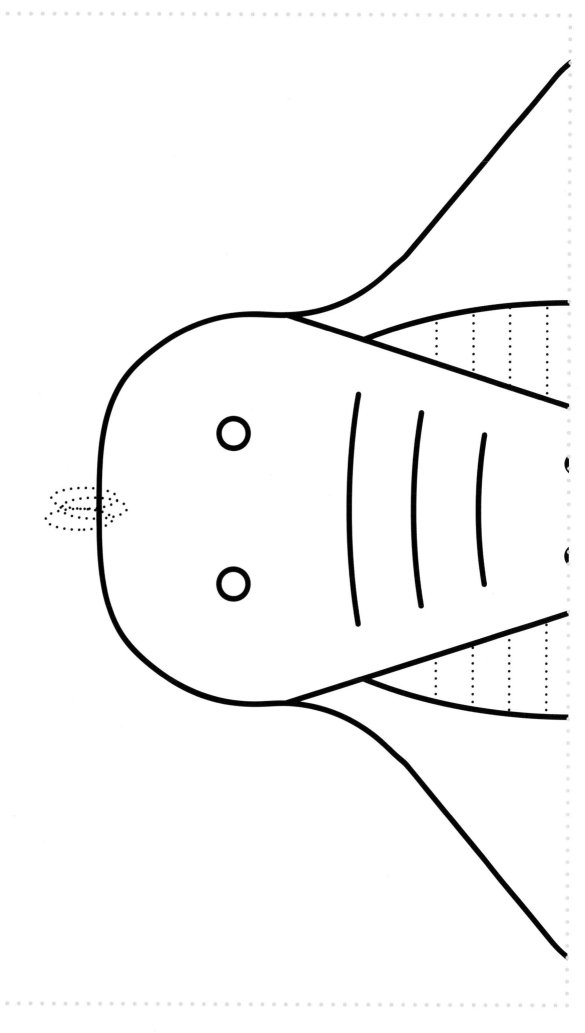

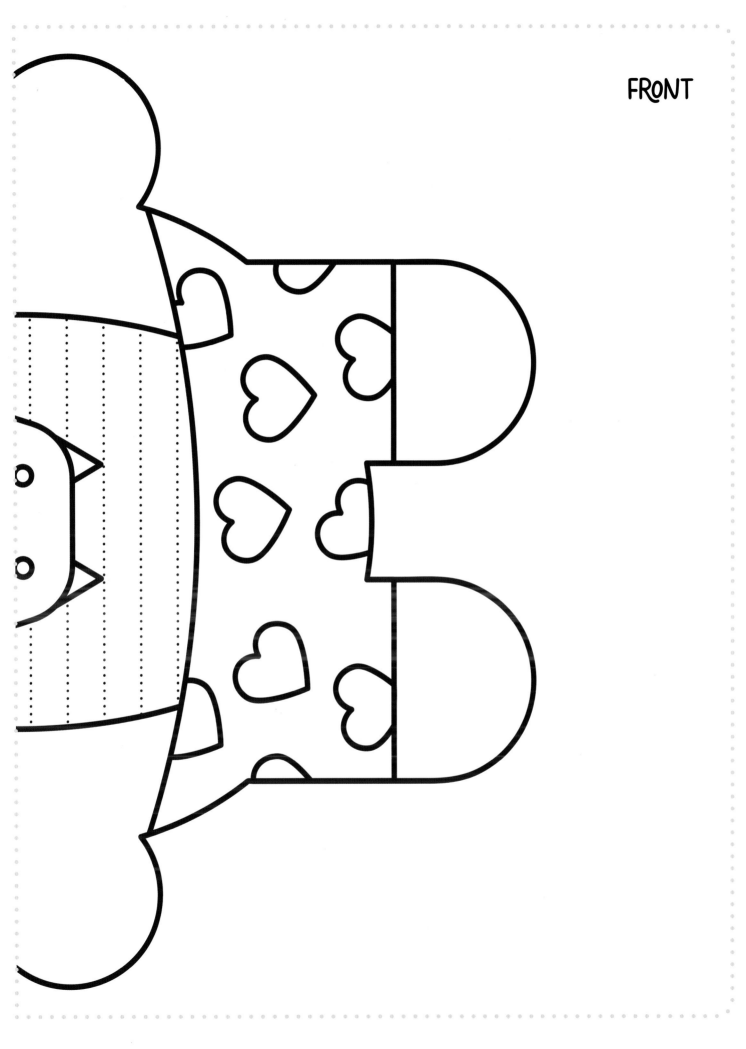

FRONT

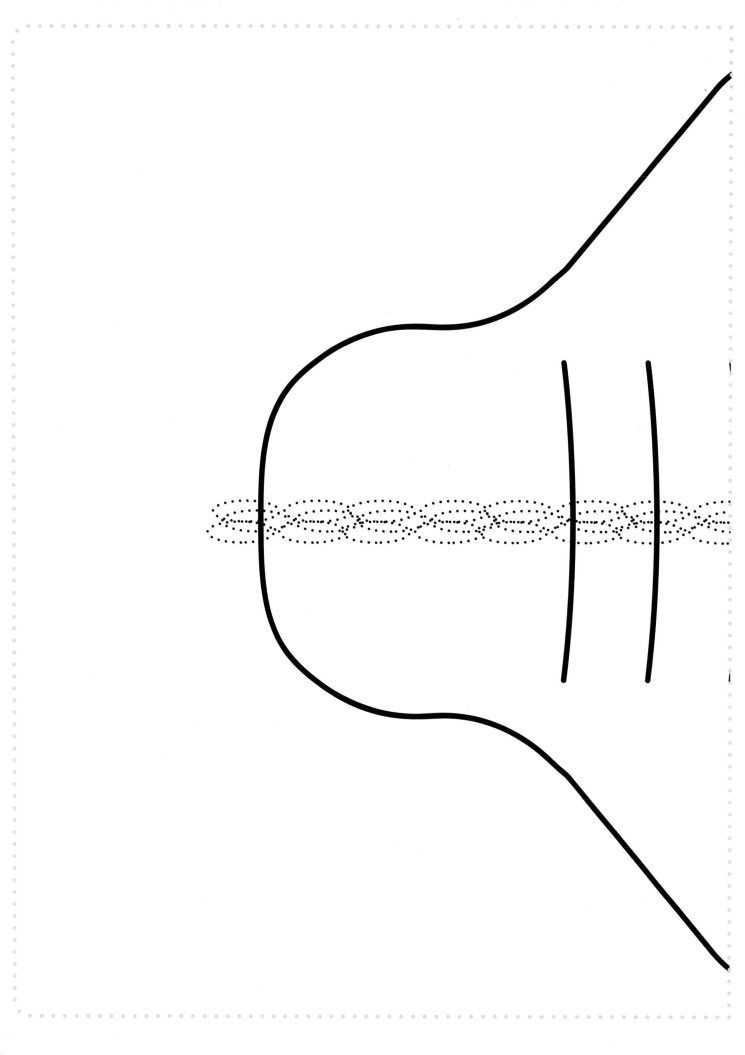

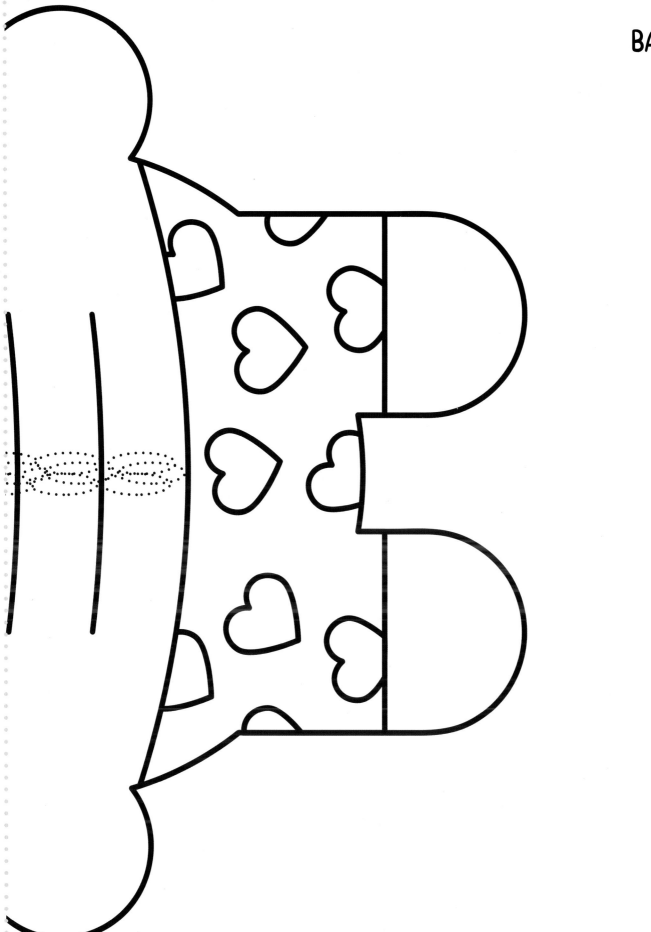

CARLOTA COW

Carlota has the most melodic and in-tune 'mooooo' you've ever heard. The rancher and the rest of the animals at Granja Paraíso were mesmerized the first time they heard this cute cow sing and got together to enter her in a singing contest. Carlota is very shy and modest, though – she would never have signed up on her own. The judges couldn't believe their ears and instantly gave Carlota first prize. That small, local contest was the start of her career as a singer. She even managed to get on the famous reality show, *Farm's Got Talent*, and won that as well! Nowadays, she travels the world singing as the leader of an Argentine lyrical-folk-style band called Paraíso, in honour of her friends who believed in her.

MATERIALS

- Medium punch needle (3mm diameter), 3cm/1⅛in length, for the face, nostrils, body, hooves and red lines on the poncho.
- Medium long punch needle (3mm diameter), 6cm/2⅜in length or work XL loops, for the snout and udders.
- Adjustable fine punch needle (2mm diameter), 2.5cm/1in length, for the poncho, poncho fringes and final contours.
- Panama fabric or similar, with 5 holes per cm (⅜in).
- Aran (US 4 medium, worsted) yarn: white for the face, body, nostrils and ears; brown for the fur markings; pink for the snout, hooves and udders; red for the poncho lines and pom-pom.
- 4 ply, baby (US 2 fine, fingering) yarn: yellow for the poncho and its fringes; burgundy for the poncho and its fringes.
- Golden embroidery silk or shiny yarn: for the final contours.
- Plastic eyes.

EMBROIDERY

FRONT

1. Snout: pom-pom.
2. Udders: pom-pom.
3. Nostrils: stem stitch.
4. Yellow fringe: fringe.
5. Burgundy fringe: fringe.
6. Yellow poncho: loops.
7. Red and burgundy poncho: loops.
8. Face: flat stitch.
9. Fur, background: flat stitch.
10. Fur, markings: flat stitch.
11. Hooves: flat stitch.
12. Hooves and snout contours: flat stitch.

BACK

13. Yellow fringe: fringe.
14. Burgundy fringe: fringe.
15. Yellow poncho: loops.
16. Red and burgundy poncho: loops.
17. Fur, background: flat stitch.
18. Fur, markings: flat stitch.
19. Hooves: flat stitch.
20. Hooves contours: flat stitch

EXTRAS

- Embroider ears separately.
- Make a pom-pom for the poncho.

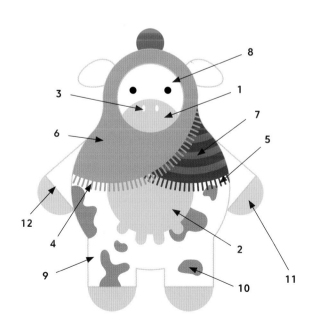

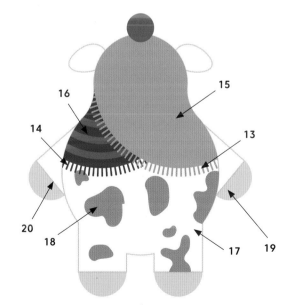

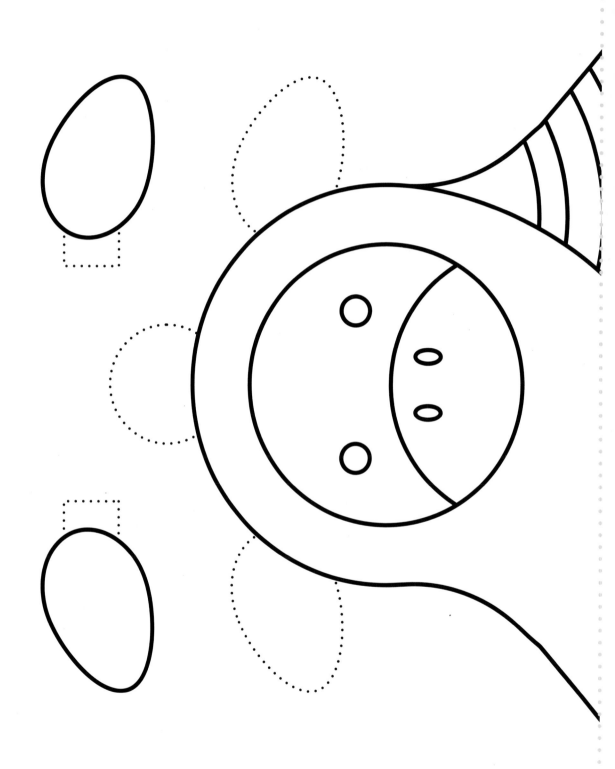

FRONT

BACK

DOMINGO DOG

Some 23 years ago, on New Year's Eve, Domingo had an accident: a truck ran him over while he was running along the road. He'd been frightened by the noise of fireworks. That night, Domingo saw his whole life flash before him in a few seconds, saw his loved ones on the journey and stared at the light. It was like looking directly at the sun. Miraculously, his body went back, but his little eyes stayed there. Today, he is a blind dog with psychic abilities. He barks at the sound of trucks and wags his tail at invisible beings. Domingo almost passed into the afterlife, but he was saved. Or not. Nobody knows for sure. He is more than 30 years old, which is weird for a dog.

MATERIALS

- Medium punch needle (3mm diameter), 3cm/1⅛in length, for the face, body (spaces between fringes) and paws.
- Adjustable fine punch needle (2mm diameter), 4cm/1⅝in length, for the snout and fringes.
- Panama fabric or similar, with 5 holes per cm (⅜in).
- Aran (US 4 medium, worsted) yarn: white for the face, body (spaces between fringes) and paws.
- 4 ply, baby (US 2 fine, fingering) yarn: white for the snout and fringes.
- Plastic nose.

EMBROIDERY

FRONT
1. Snout: pom-pom.
2. Long fur: fringe.
3. Face, body (spaces between fringes) and paws: flat stitch.

BACK
4. Long fur: fringe.
5. Back (spaces between fringes) and paws: flat stitch.

EXTRAS
- You can sew the fringes above the nose down, so that they stay put.

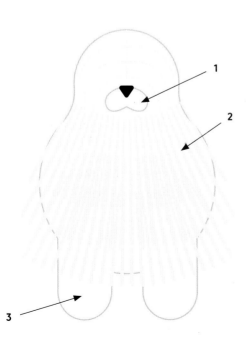

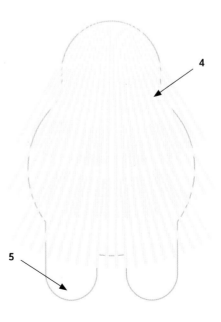

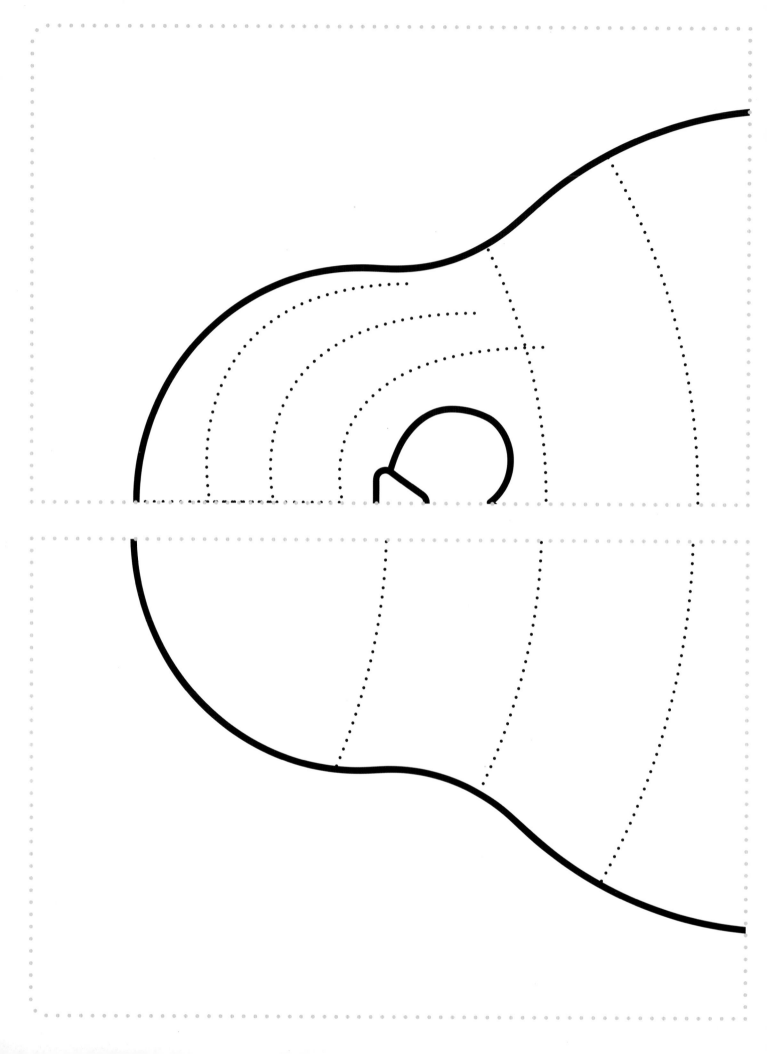

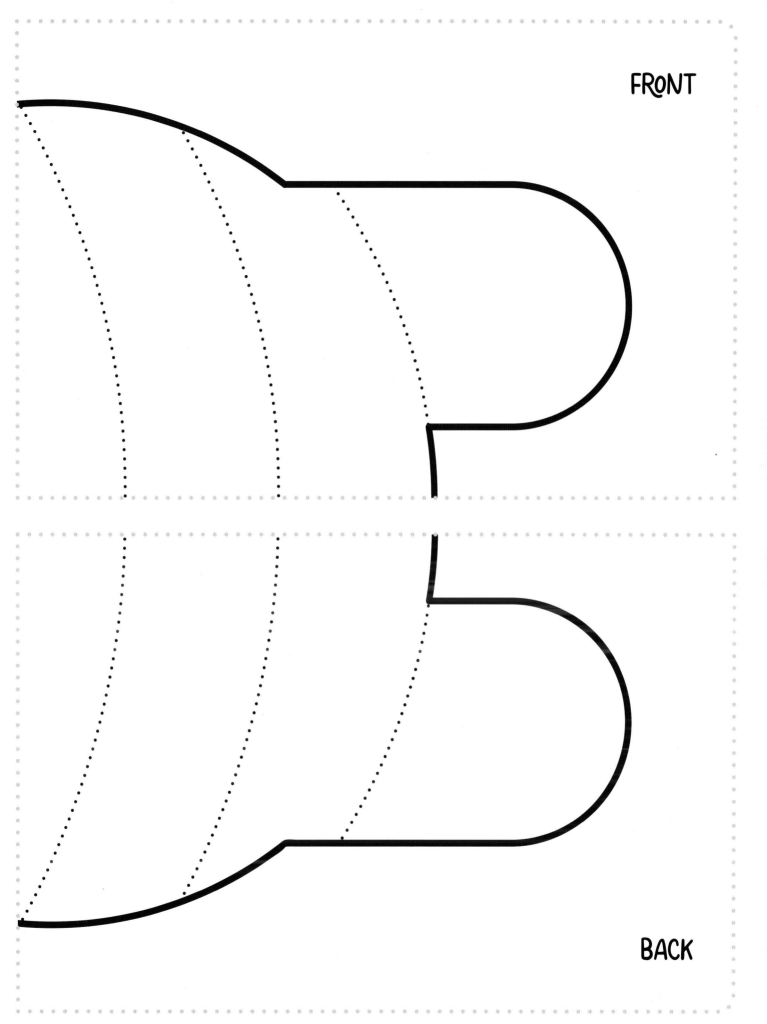

FRONT

BACK

ENRIQUE ELEPHANT

Enrique was unlucky at interviews and the jobs he got didn't last long. His large size made him feel clumsy. When he was a waiter, he could handle the tray very well with his trunk, but his thundering footsteps caused plates to fall and wine to spill from the glasses, splashing onto the customers' clothes.

Every job ended in failure ... until last Tuesday. He was walking along and heard frightened screams. A little brown bear was drowning. Enrique stuck his trunk into the water and sucked it all up, saving the bear's life. Today, Enrique is the only lifeguard who cannot swim, but then he doesn't need to!

MATERIALS

- Medium punch needle (3mm diameter), 3cm/1⅛in length, for all but fine details.
- Adjustable fine punch needle (2mm diameter), 4cm/1⅝in length, for the final contours.
- Panama fabric or similar, with 5 holes per cm (⅜in).
- Aran (US 4 medium, worsted) yarn: dark grey for the body and ears; light grey for the chest; white for the tusks; dark yellow for the swimsuit; light yellow for the decorative lines.
- Silver embroidery silk or shiny yarn: for the final contours of the chest.
- Thick cord: for the wrapped cord for the trunk.
- Plastic eyes.

EMBROIDERY

FRONT
1. Trunk: wrapped cord.
2. Chest: flat stitch.
3. Face and body: flat stitch.
4. Tusks: flat stitch.
5. Swimwear: flat stitch.
6. Swimwear lines: satin stitch.
7. Chest contours: flat stitch.

BACK
8. Body: flat stitch.
9. Swimwear: flat stitch.
10. Swimwear line: satin stitch.

EXTRAS
- Embroider ears separately.

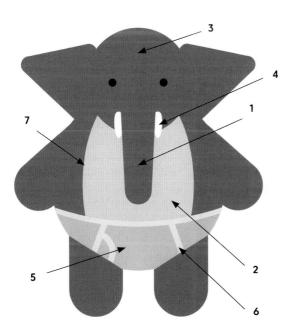

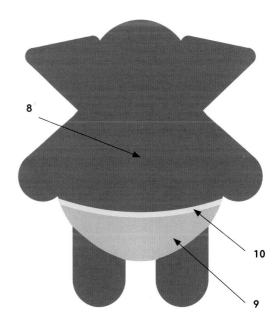

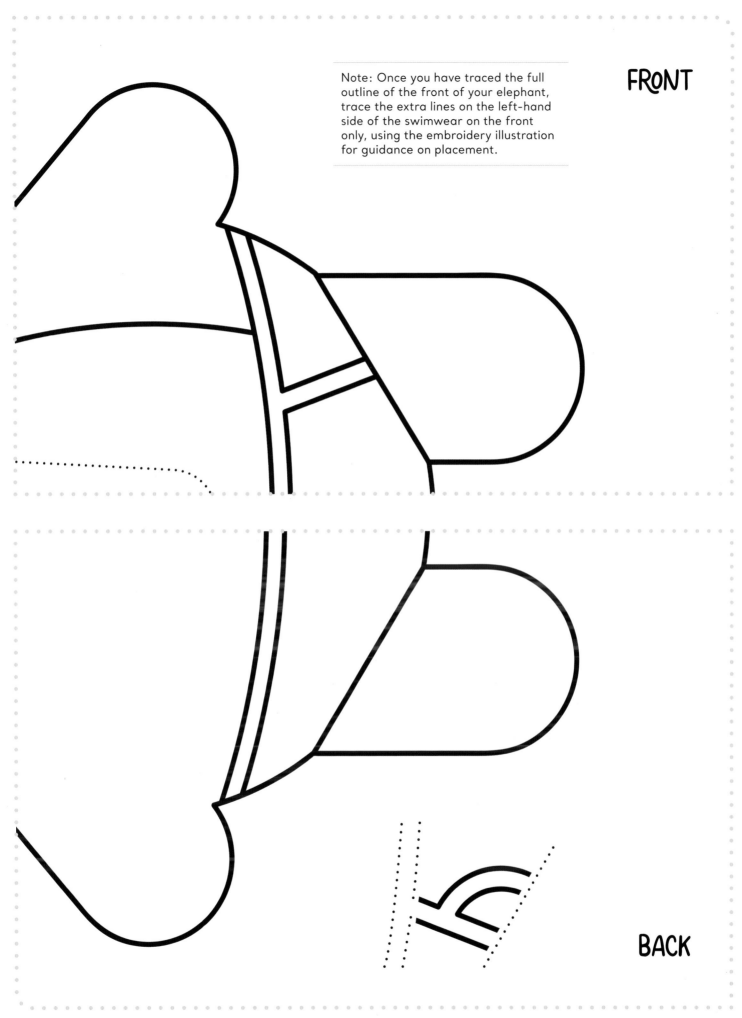

Note: Once you have traced the full outline of the front of your elephant, trace the extra lines on the left-hand side of the swimwear on the front only, using the embroidery illustration for guidance on placement.

BACK

FELIPE FOX

Have you heard? Foxes are actually very clever. It's true! Felipe is a millionaire fox. You're probably wondering how a fox made so much money. Well, Felipe patented his own image and the word 'Fox'. As a result, he receives large sums in royalties every month from human businesspeople around the world who need his permission to use his image in the logos and names of their companies, such as fashion brands, an Internet search engine and a TV channel. Felipe knows that the businesspeople did not copy his image (actually, the Internet search engine's logo looks more like his cousin Francisco), but he also knows that humans do not distinguish between one fox and another.

MATERIALS

- Medium punch needle (3mm diameter), 3cm/1⅛in length, for the hat and paws.
- Adjustable fine punch needle (2mm diameter), 2.5cm/1in length, for the body, face and final contours.
- Adjustable fine punch needle (2mm diameter), 4cm/1⅝in length, for the tail.
- Panama fabric or similar, with 5 holes per cm (⅜in).
- Aran (US 4 medium, worsted) yarn: black for the paws and two shades of blue for the hat.
- 4 ply, baby (US 2 fine, fingering) yarn: two shades of orange for the body, face and tail; white for the tummy, snout and tail.
- Golden embroidery silk or shiny yarn: for the final contours of the face.
- Plastic eyes and nose.

EMBROIDERY

FRONT
1. Body and tummy: brushed loop.
2. Hat: loop.
3. Hat contour: stem stitch.
4. Snout and mouth lines: flat stitch.
5. Face: flat stitch.
6. Paws: flat stitch.
7. Face contours: flat stitch.

BACK
8. Body: brushed loop.
9. Tail: pom-pom.
10. Hat: loop.
11. Paws: flat stitch.

EXTRAS
- Make pom-poms for hat ties.
- Hat ties: using a wool needle, make a long stitch in and out each side of the neck and attach a pom-pom to each end.

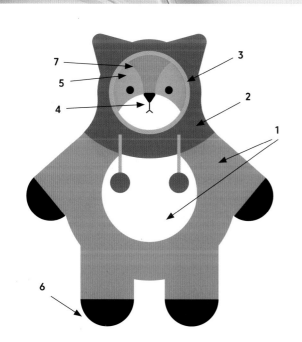

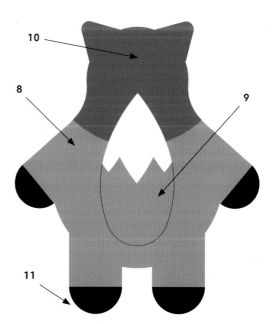

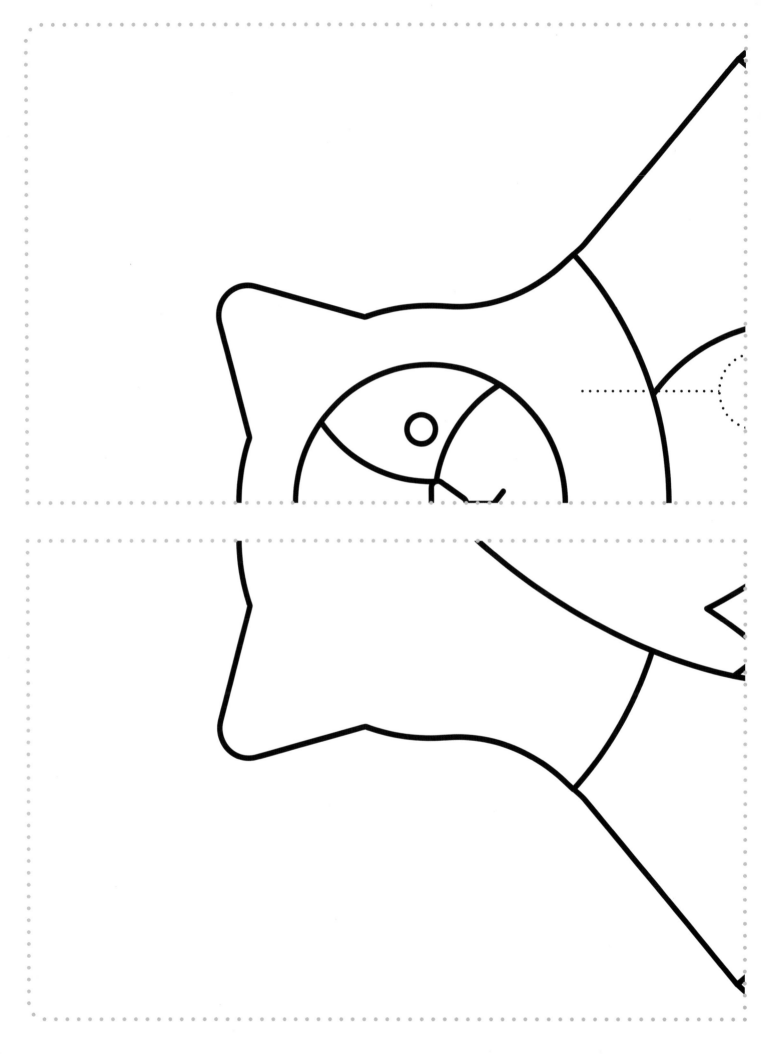

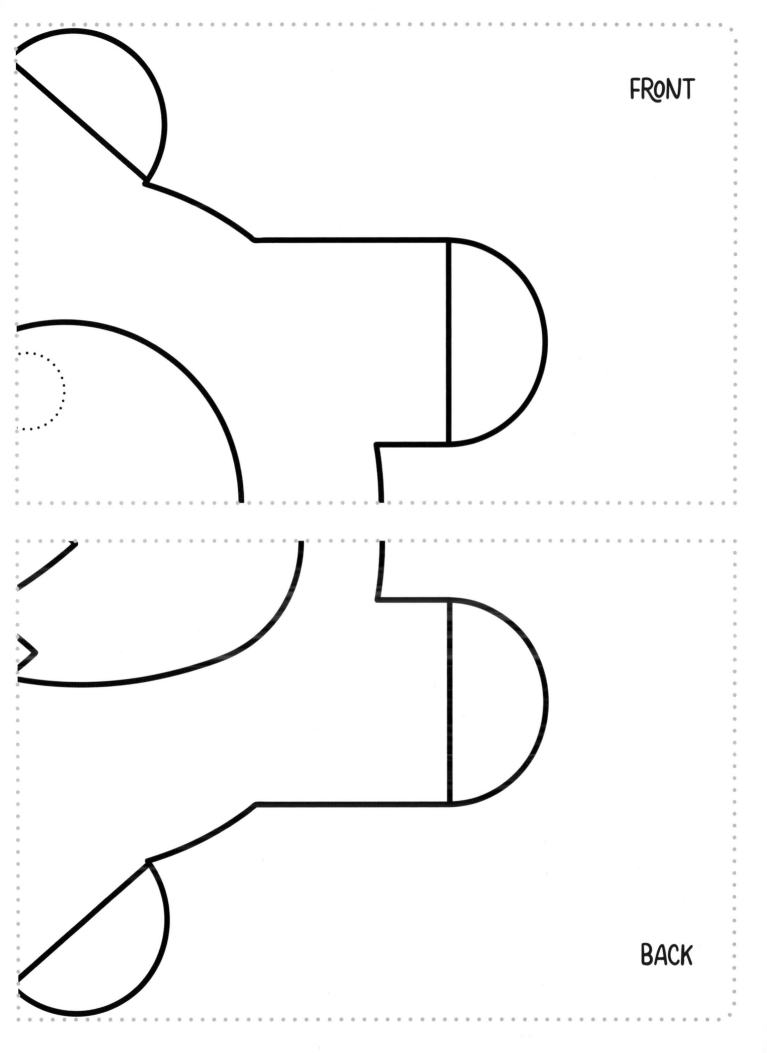

FRONT

BACK

GASPAR GIRAFFE

Gaspar is in trouble. Tonight he is on an important mission, his first one. He is going to debut as an associate for the Savannah Secret Service Agency. His instructions are to go to a fancy party that the billionaire and mysterious Black Snake is putting on, blend in with his guests and sneak into his study to find evidence of corruption and illegal deals. Gaspar's bow tie has a small, hidden camera, but he's already regretting taking the job and lying in his application. He said he was a zebra. 'It is going to be a bit difficult for me to "blend in" and "sneak" into the study, given that I am a tall giraffe', he thought.

MATERIALS

- Medium punch needle (3mm diameter), 3cm/1⅛in length, for the fur, hooves, face, shirt bib front and rose.
- Medium long punch needle (3mm diameter), 6cm/2⅜in length or work XL loops, for the snout and bow tie.
- Adjustable fine punch needle (2mm diameter), 4cm/1⅝in length, for the final contours of the chest and face.
- Panama fabric or similar, with 5 holes per cm (⅜in).
- Aran (US 4 medium, worsted) yarn: two shades of yellow for the fur and horns; white for the face, nostrils and shirt bib; brown for the snout and ears; black for the bow tie, shirt bib front pintuck lines and hooves; red for the rose.
- Golden embroidery silk or shiny yarn: for the final contours of chest.
- Plastic eyes.
- Plastic buttons for the shirt bib front.

EMBROIDERY

FRONT

1. Snout and nostrils: pom-pom.
2. Bow tie: pom-pom.
3. Light yellow fur: flat stitch.
4. Dark yellow fur markings: flat stitch.
5. Hooves: flat stitch.
6. Face: flat stitch.
7. Shirt bib front pintuck lines: flat stitch.
8. Shirt bib front background: flat stitch
9. Rose: rose stitch.
10. Shirt bib front pintuck lines: if necessary, redo with flat stitch.
11. Shirt bib front and face outlines: flat stitch.

BACK

12. Bow tie back fastening strip: pom-pom.
13. Light yellow fur: flat stitch.
14. Dark yellow fur markings: flat stitch.
15. Hooves: flat stitch.

EXTRAS

- Embroider ears and horns separately.

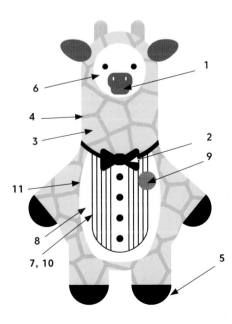

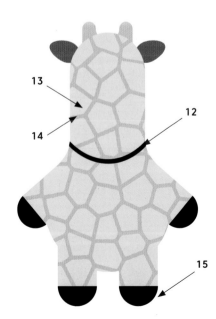

Note: you only need to trace the circle for the flower on the right side of the front. For the left front, complete the pintuck lines of the bib front of the shirt instead.

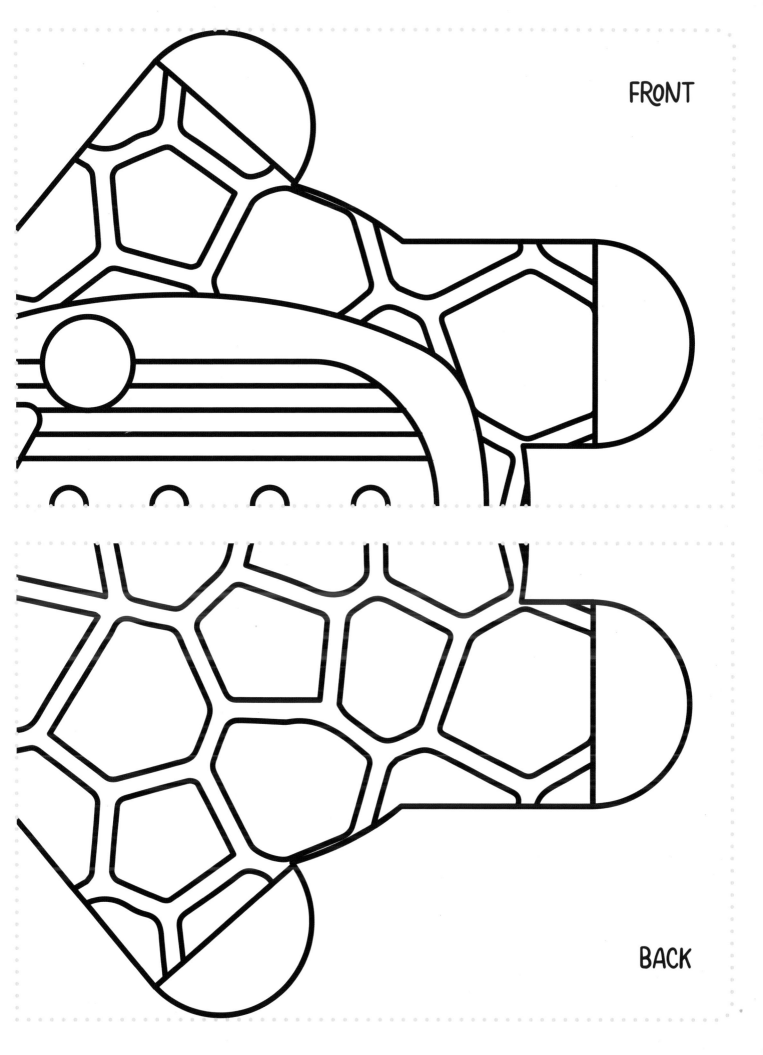

FRONT

BACK

HELENA HEN

~

Do not be fooled by appearances. That's just a façade, a disguise. Although Helena looks like a cute and harmless hen, she is actually a tenacious activist for chick rights. Everything changed after that day she read *Animal Farm* by George Orwell – a book that Mabel lent her, the hen next door. She weaves and chatters by day, but at night she pulls her shawl up over her beak to hide her identity and meets with her buddies to plan the next attack.

MATERIALS

- Medium punch needle (3mm diameter), 3cm/1⅛in length, for the body, shawl lines, chest, flowers and leaves.
- Medium long punch needle (3mm diameter), 6cm/2⅜in length or work XL loops, for the beak, comb and wattle.
- Adjustable fine punch needle (2mm diameter), 2.5cm/1in length, for the shawl, fringe and final contours.
- Panama fabric or similar, with 5 holes per cm (⅜in).
- Aran (US 4 medium, worsted) yarn: grey for the body; yellow for the beak; red for the comb, wattle and leaves; white for the chest and shawl lines; pink for the big flowers; green for the small flowers.
- 4 ply, baby (US 2 fine, fingering) yarn: blue for the shawl and fringe.
- Silver embroidery silk or shiny yarn: for the final contours of the chest and shawl.
- Plastic eyes.

EMBROIDERY

FRONT

1. Beak: pom-pom.
2. Shawl fringe: fringe.
3. Body: loops.
4. Comb: XL loops.
5. Wattle: XL loops.
6. Chest: flat stitch.
7. Shawl white lines: cross stitch line.
8. Shawl: flat stitch.
9. Knot: rose stitch.
10. Chest and shawl contours: flat stitch.

BACK

11. Shawl fringe: fringe.
12. Body: loops.
13. Small flowers: loops.
14. Big flower: rose stitch.
15. Leaves: leaf stitch.
16. Shawl white lines: cross stitch line.
17. Shawl: flat stitch.
18. Shawl contours: flat stitch.

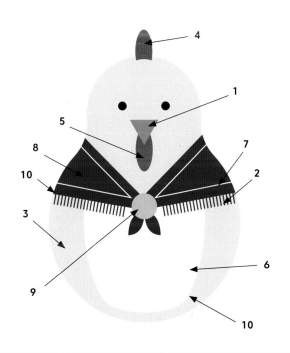

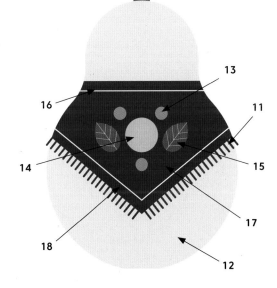

Note: Once you have traced the full outline of the back of your hen, trace the leaves and flower outlines, below left, first, placing the large flower in the centre of the shawl. Then trace the extra leaf and flower outlines, below right, using the embroidery illustration for guidance on placement.

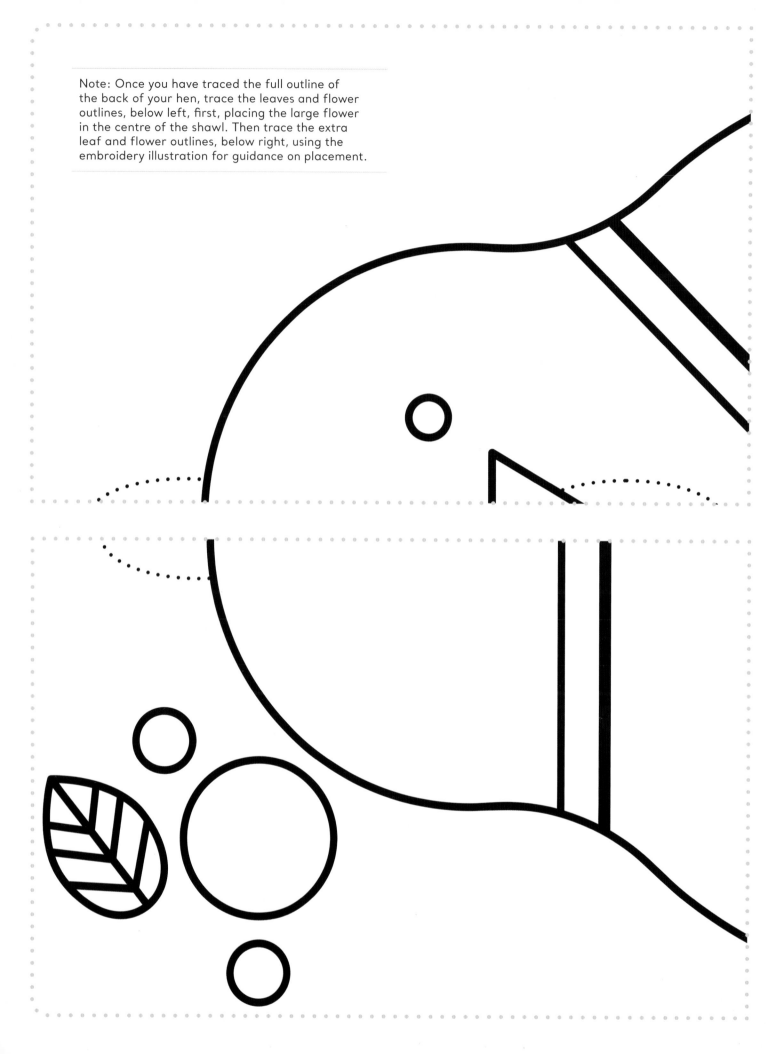

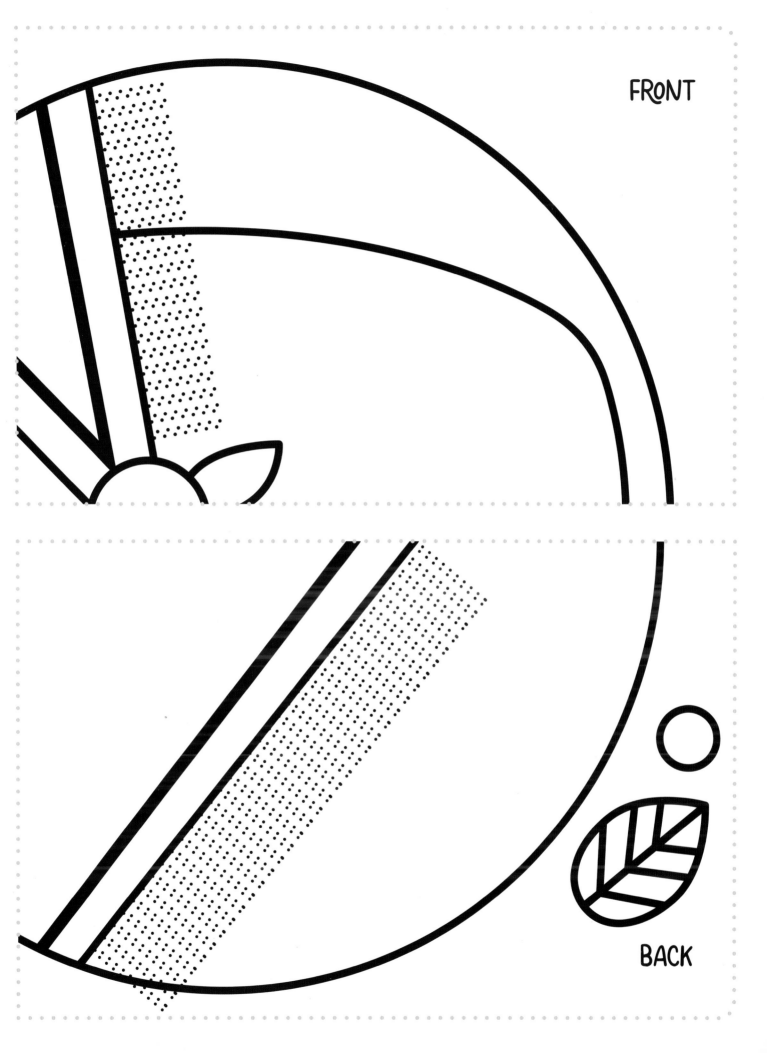

FRONT

BACK

KARIM KOALA

Karim is a teenage koala. He is trying to work out his true identity and is thinking about joining a gang. Maybe becoming a rebel is what he should do. He may also join a band. He thought about being a punk, but he is afraid to dye his hair or pierce his nose. He borrowed his older brother's DC/CA T-shirt, as it sounds like a rock band. It suits him perfectly. Now it only remains to learn their songs.

MATERIALS

- Medium punch needle (3mm diameter), 3cm/1⅛in length, for the fur and face.
- Adjustable fine punch needle (2mm diameter), 2.5cm/1in length, for the claws, chest, snout and mouth, T-shirt and its logo, and final contours.
- Adjustable fine punch needle (2mm diameter), 4cm/1⅝in length, for the nose.
- Panama fabric or similar, with 5 holes per cm (⅜in).
- DK (US 3 light, DK, light worsted) yarn: dark grey for the fur and ears; light grey for the face.
- 4 ply, baby (US 2 fine, fingering) yarn: black for the claws, T-shirt, nose and mouth; white for the snout, chest and logo.
- Silver embroidery silk or shiny yarn: for the final contours of the snout and T-shirt.
- Plastic eyes.

EMBROIDERY

FRONT
1. Nose: pom-pom.
2. Fur: tufting.
3. Claws: loops.
4. Chest: loops.
5. Mouth: flat stitch.
6. Face and snout: flat stitch.
7. T-shirt: flat stitch.
8. Logo: flat stitch.
9. Snout and T-shirt contours: flat stitch.
10. Mouth: if necessary, redo with flat stitch.

BACK
11. Fur: tufting.
12. Claws: loops.
13. T-shirt: flat stitch.
14. T-shirt contours: flat stitch.

EXTRAS
- Make big pom-poms for ears.

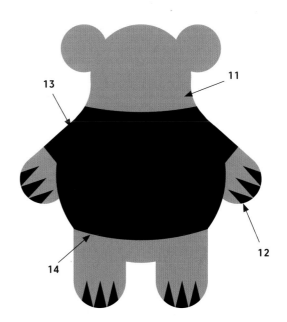

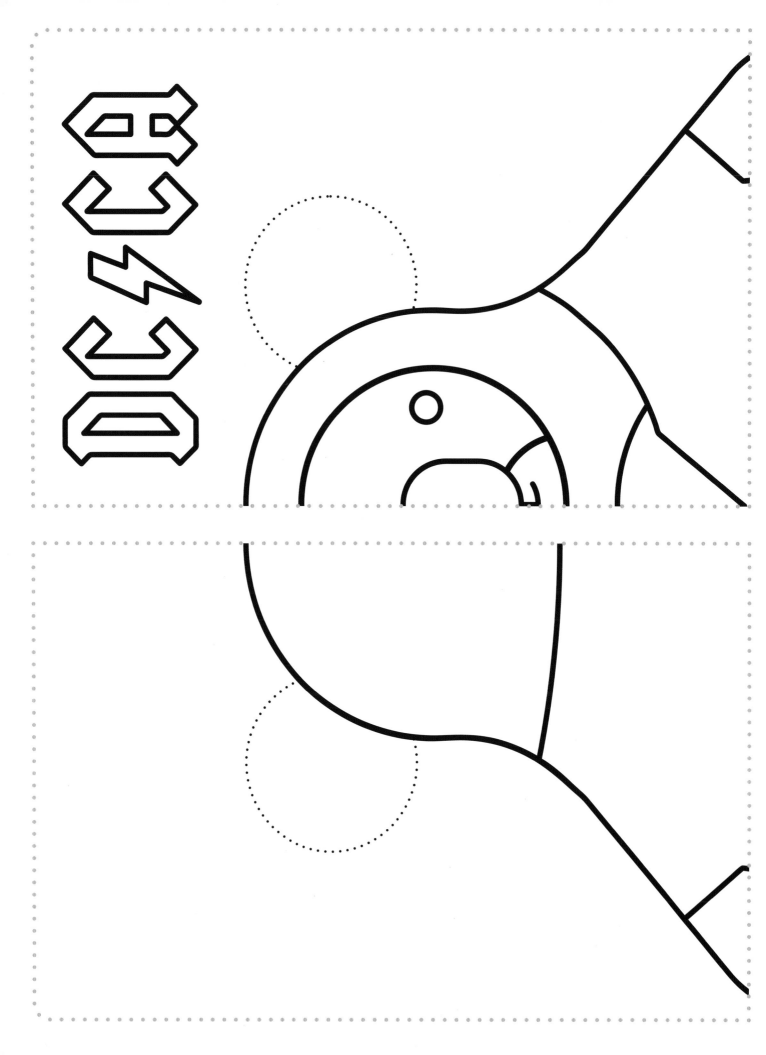

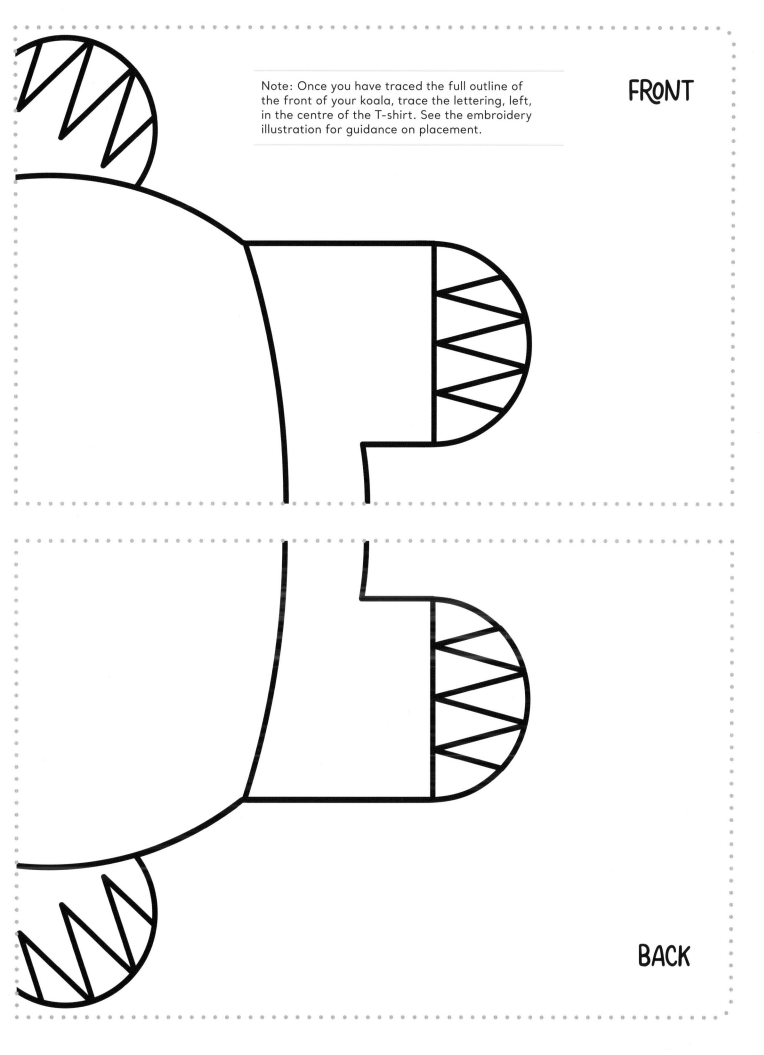

Note: Once you have traced the full outline of the front of your koala, trace the lettering, left, in the centre of the T-shirt. See the embroidery illustration for guidance on placement.

BACK

LEONARDO LION

Tired of the pressure of being King of the Savannah (and mediating in neighbours' disputes, solving problems and those boring diplomatic dinners), one morning Leonardo packed his things and escaped in search of a more peaceful life. He walked and walked for months, with his backpack on his shoulder, until he reached a place where no one would ever find him: the Patagonia forests. Today, he is a relaxed forest ranger, who spends his time making soups, looking out of the window of his cabin and collecting logs for the fire he starts at sunset. As he blows the steam from his hot soup, he rejoices, glad to have left behind the chaos of the Savannah.

MATERIALS

- Medium punch needle (3mm diameter), 3cm/1⅛in length, for the mane, face, paws, lower body and shoes.
- Adjustable fine punch needle (2mm diameter), 2cm/¾in length, for the shirt.
- Panama fabric or similar, with 5 holes per cm (⅜in).
- DK (US 3 light, DK, light worsted) yarn: brown for the mane and shoes; white for the snout; yellow for the face, ears, paws and lower body.
- 4 ply, baby (US 2 fine, fingering) yarn: three shades of red for the shirt; black for the mouth.
- Golden embroidery silk or shiny yarn: for the final contours of the snout and shoes.
- Plastic eyes and nose.
- Plastic buttons for the shirt.

EMBROIDERY

FRONT
1. Mane: loops, brushed.
2. Shirt: loops.
3. Mouth: flat stitch.
4. Snout: flat stitch.
5. Face: flat stitch.
6. Lower body: flat stitch.
7. Shoes: flat stitch.
8. Snout and shoe contours: flat stitch.
9. Mouth: if necessary, redo with flat stitch.

BACK
10. Mane: loops, brushed.
11. Shirt: loops.
12. Lower body: flat stitch.
13. Shoes: flat stitch.
14. Shoe contours: flat stitch.

EXTRAS
- Make pom-poms for ears.
- Sew buttons on shirt.

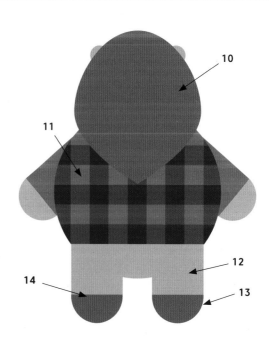

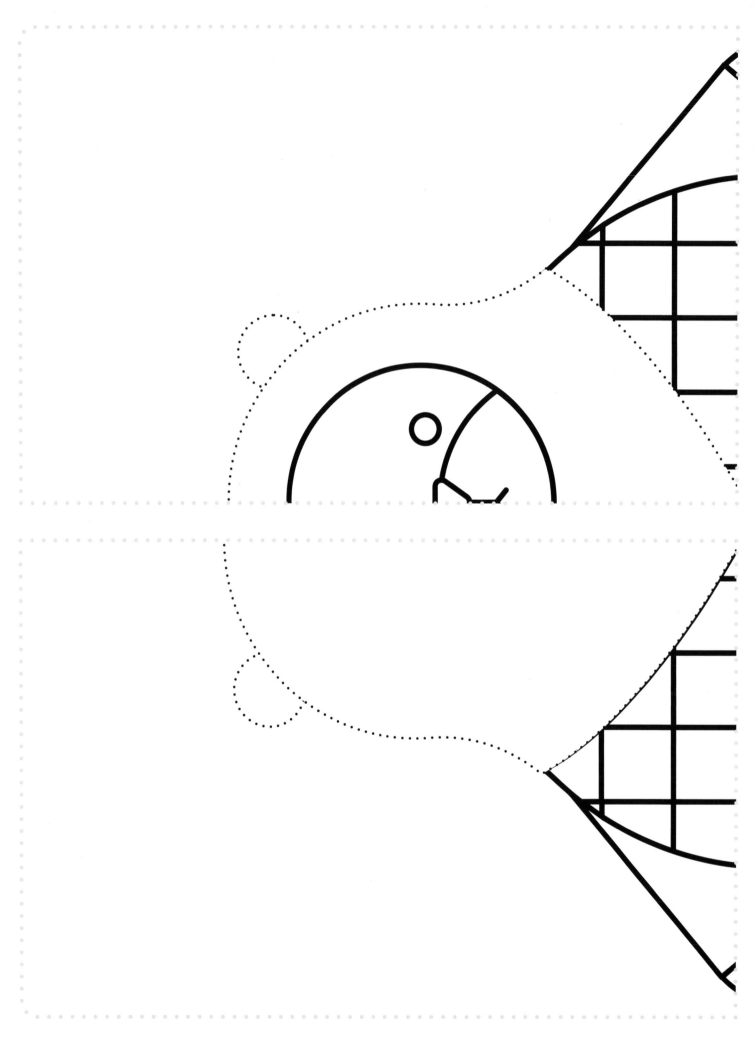

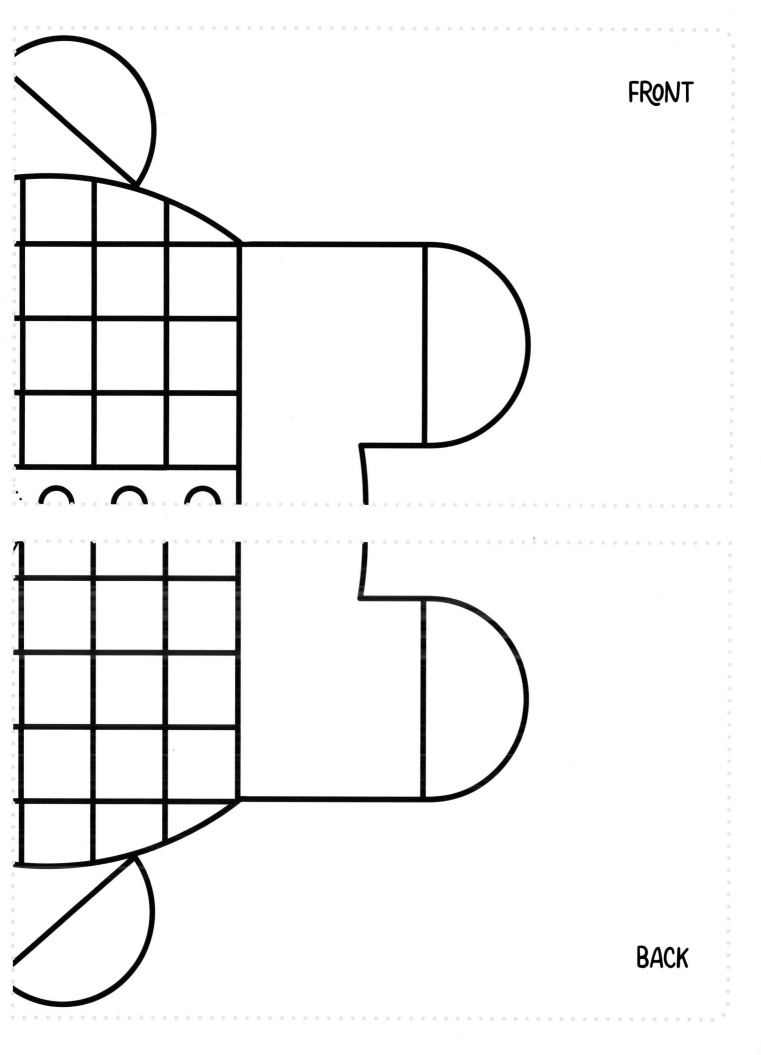

FRONT

BACK

LUCIO LEOPARD

Lucio is a talented hair stylist, an expert in creating wild looks, thanks to his skills with scissors and hair colours. Not liking to stay anywhere for long, he loves seeing new places, making friends along the way, and he gets on with all animals. He has attended major fashion shows around the world and participated in photo shoots for well-known clothing brands, but there is mystery surrounding Lucio. Urban legend has it that he is not a leopard, that he uses his abilities to transform himself. There are claims that he has been seen in the form of a lion, with long, mane-like hair extensions, and as a panther, with his fur dyed entirely black. At one point, someone said that they saw him looking like a cheetah, but he was not very fast. What will Lucio be next?

MATERIALS

- Medium punch needle (3mm diameter), 3cm/1⅛in length, for the pocket and sleeveless jacket.

- Adjustable fine punch needle (2mm diameter), 2cm/¾in length, for the fur and tummy.

- Adjustable fine punch needle (2mm diameter), 4cm/1⅝in length, for the snout, jacket art on the back and final contour of the tummy.

- Panama fabric or similar, with 5 holes per cm (⅜in).

- DK (US 3 light, DK, light worsted) yarn: denim blue for the sleeveless jacket; dark blue for the pocket.

- 4 ply, baby (US 2 fine, fingering) yarn: brown, black and yellow for the fur and ears; white for the snout, tummy and banner on back; red for the heart.

- Golden embroidery silk or shiny yarn: for the final contour of the tummy.

- Plastic eyes and nose.

EMBROIDERY

FRONT
1. Snout: pom-pom.
2. Black fur markings: loops, short.
3. Brown fur markings: loops, short.
4. Yellow fur: loops, short.
5. Pocket: loops.
6. Sleeveless jacket: loops.
7. Tummy: flat stitch.
8. Tummy contour: flat stitch.

BACK
9. Black fur markings: loops, short.
10. Brown fur markings: loops, short.
11. Yellow fur: loops, short.
12. Banner: loops.
13. Heart: loops.
14. Sleeveless jacket: loops.

EXTRAS
- Make pom-poms for ears.

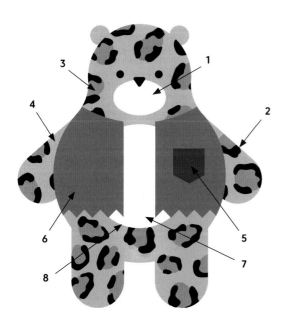

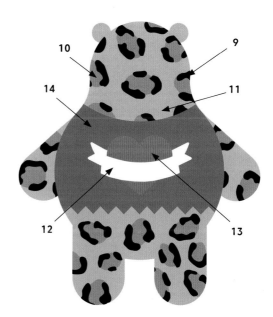

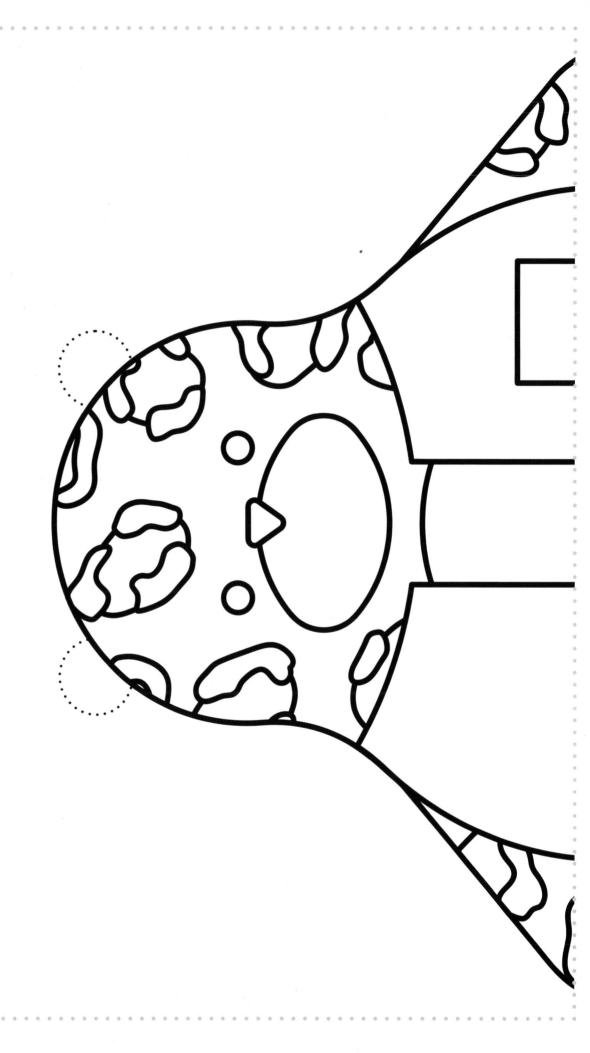

FRONT

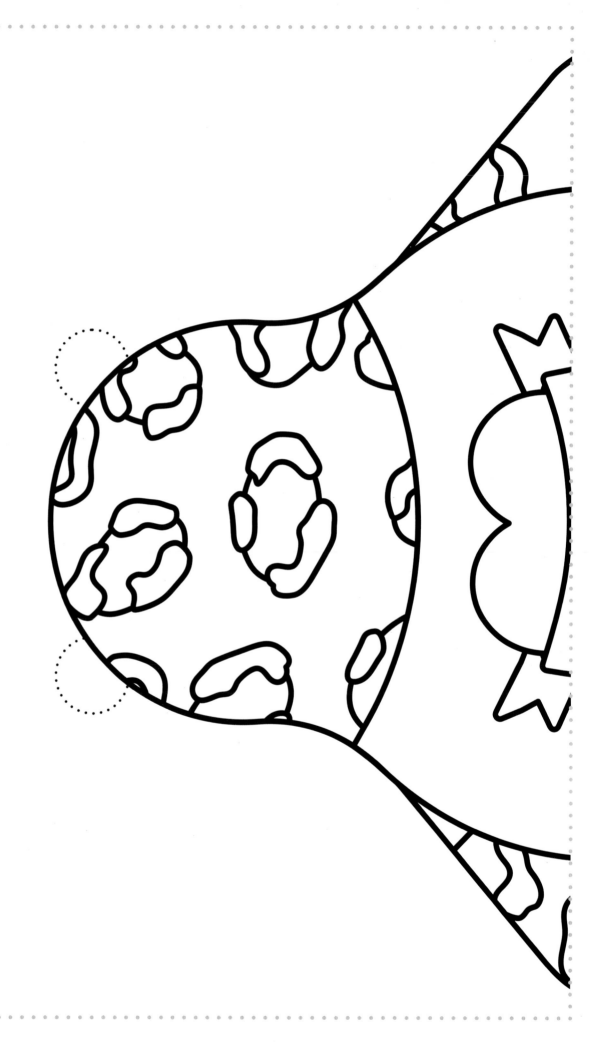

MATEO MONKEY

Mateo is the host of a travel TV show. It's not very long and it's not prime-time TV, but he is proud of it. He works very hard, does research on the places he is going to visit, films and edits the videos, then delivers them to the channel, which airs his work on Sundays. His slot is about 10 to 15 minutes long. For each new programme, Mateo prepares his suitcase, passport and, of course, he cannot live without his warm puffer jacket, as he always works at night. That's because his specialism is night tourism – theatre, festivals, nightclubs, guided visits to cemeteries, walks in the moonlight ... He is an albino monkey, so he can't go out during the day – the sun hurts him – but he's turned it into a positive.

MATERIALS

- Medium punch needle (3mm diameter), 3cm/1⅛in length, for the face, ears, paws and belly and jacket.

- Adjustable fine punch needle (2mm diameter), 3cm/1⅛in length, for the fur, mouth and final contours.

- Panama fabric or similar, with 5 holes per cm (⅜in).

- DK (US 3 light, DK, light worsted) yarn: burgundy for the jacket collar; red for the jacket; nude for the skin.

- 4 ply, baby (US 2 fine, fingering) yarn: white for the fur; black for the mouth.

- Shiny yarn: for the final contours of the jacket.

- Plastic eyes and tiny eyes for nostrils.

EMBROIDERY

FRONT

1. Fur: loops.
2. Mouth: flat stitch.
3. Face, ears, paws and belly: flat stitch.
4. Jacket: fill stitch stripes.
5. Jacket collar: flat stitch.
6. Zip: flat stitch.
7. Jacket contours: flat stitch.
8. Belly button: knot tied in nude yarn.
9. Mouth: if necessary, embroider it again with flat stitch.

BACK

10. Fur: loops.
11. Ears and paws: flat stitch.
12. Jacket: fill stitch stripes.
13. Jacket collar: flat stitch.
14. Jacket contours: flat stitch.

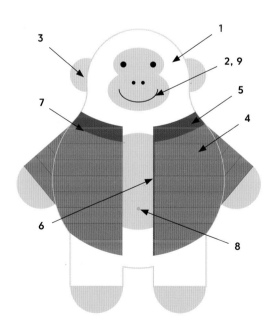

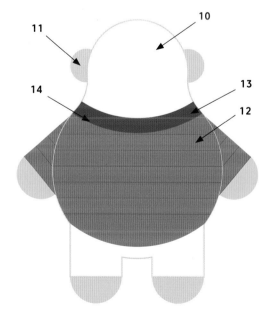

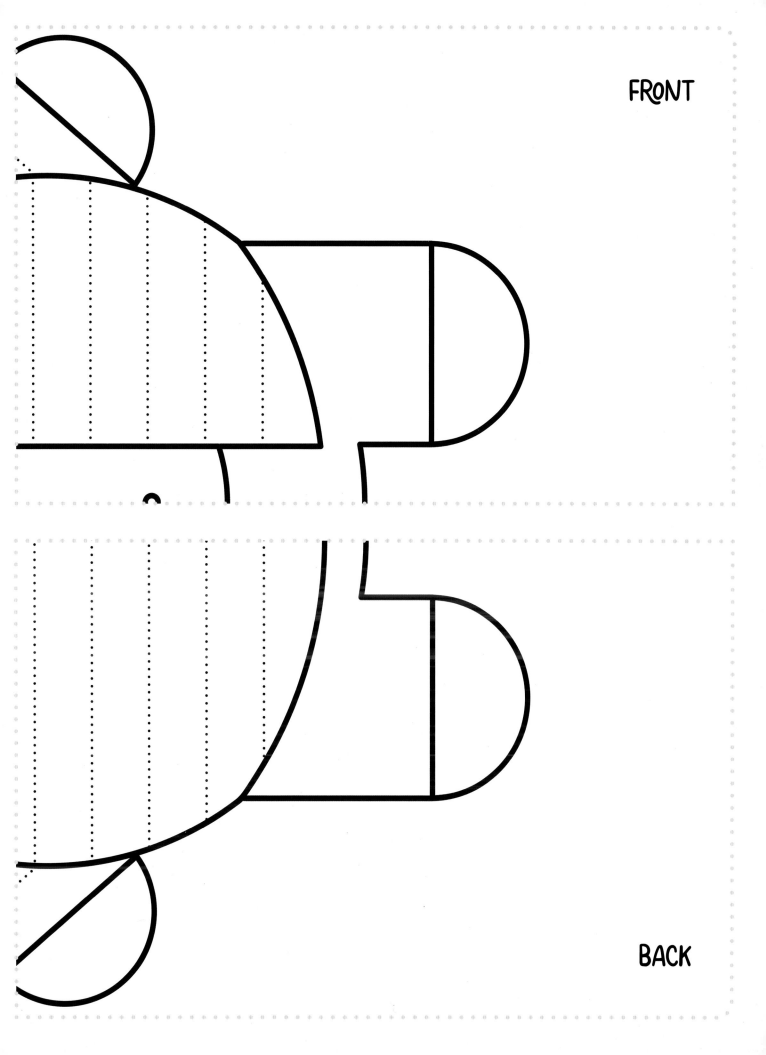

FRONT

BACK

PABLO PANDA

Pablo has a secret. He has been living in a panda community for a long time but, in fact, he is not a panda. He is a black bear with vitiligo. One day, years ago, he woke up in his den and his mum had gone. She never came back, but he was found by some friendly pandas who took him to live with them in their community. Time passed and it became more and more difficult for the pandas to tell him the truth. He thinks he is a panda, feels at home with them, loves sugar cane, boasts about being an endangered species and enjoys being looked after by the conservationsts – it's as though he were living in a spa. Also, he is the least clumsy one in his group, which has made him a bit of a leader, so he feels good. Let's keep his secret, OK? Shh ...

MATERIALS

- Medium punch needle (3mm diameter), 3cm/1⅛in length, for the face, body, eyes, belt and braces.
- Adjustable fine punch needle (2mm diameter), 4cm/1⅝in length, for the snout, paws and final contours.
- Panama fabric or similar, with 5 holes per cm (⅜in).
- DK (US 3 light, DK, light worsted) yarn: black and white for the face, body, ears, tail and belt buckle; dark green for the shorts; light green for the belt and braces.
- 4 ply, baby (US 2 fine, fingering) yarn: white for the snout; dark grey for the paws.
- Silver embroidery silk or shiny yarn: for the final contours of the face.
- Plastic nose.

EMBROIDERY

FRONT
1. Snout: pom-pom.
2. Paws: pom-pom.
3. Belt buckle: stem stitch.
4. Shorts: loops.
5. Face and body: flat stitch.
6. Eyes: flat stitch.
7. Belt and braces: satin stitch.
8. Tummy and face contours: flat stitch.

BACK
9. Shorts: loops.
10. Body: flat stitch.
11. Belt and braces: satin stitch.

EXTRAS
- Make pom-poms for ears and tail.

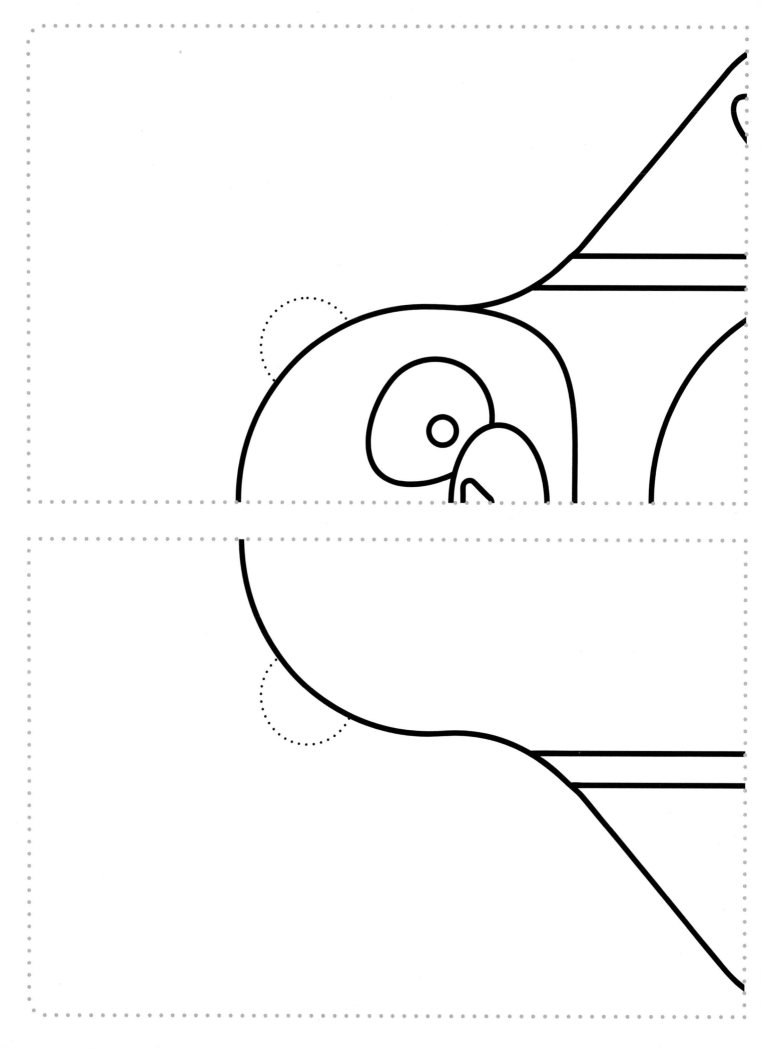

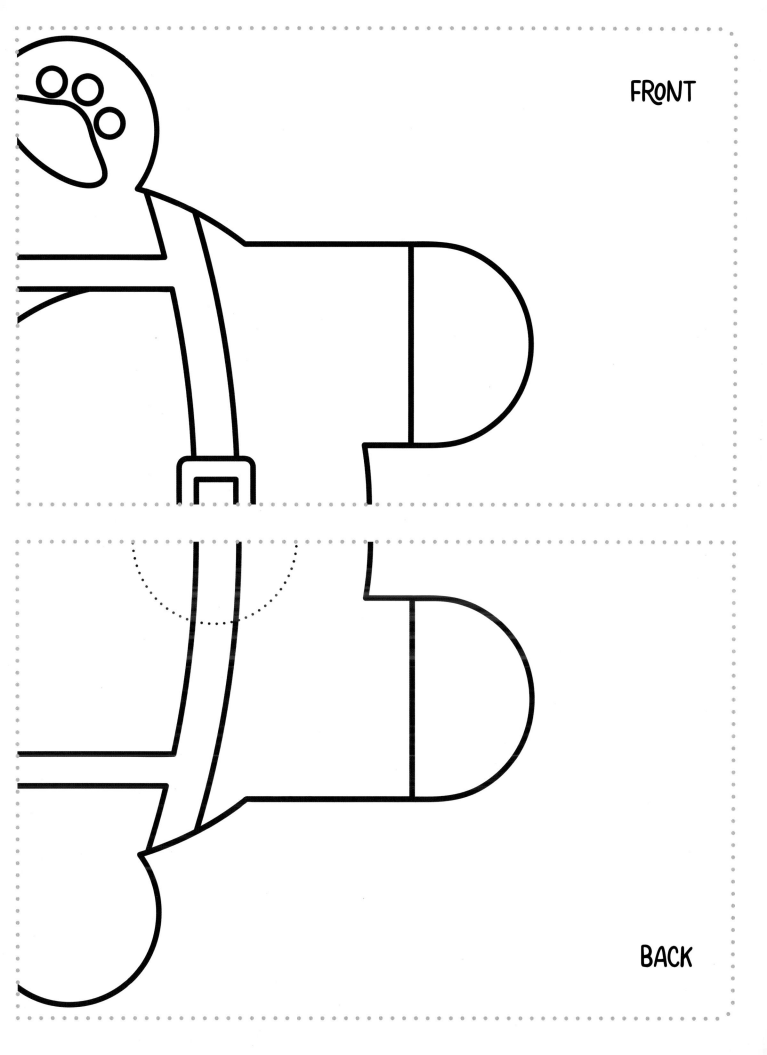

FRONT

BACK

PATRICIO PENGUIN

Patricio is a penguin who feels the cold. He can't leave his little cave without his scarf and hat. Sometimes he even needs a blanket. How can a penguin not like the cold? Well, Patricio was born in captivity. The zoo did all it could, but the temperatures never quite matched those of the Antarctic and he got used to it being warmer. One night, after years of planning to escape because the children staring at him through the glass gave him nightmares, Patricio, along with his parents and some of his cousins, succeeded. Today, they live on Half Moon Island in Antarctica. Patricio is always cold, but it's worth it as there are no people for miles around!

MATERIALS

- Medium punch needle (3mm diameter), 3cm/1⅛in length, for the face, body, hat contour and stripes in the scarf.

- Medium long punch needle (3mm diameter), 6cm/2⅜in length or work XL loops, for the beak and dark part of the hat.

- Adjustable fine punch needle (2mm diameter), 4cm/1⅝in length, for the scarf fringes and final contours.

- Panama fabric or similar, with 5 holes per cm (⅜in).

- Aran (US 4 medium, worsted) yarn: black and white for the body and face ; light blue for the scarf; two shades of yellow for the hat and beak.

- 4 ply, baby (US 2 fine, fingering) yarn: dark yellow forthe scarf fringes.

- Silk or shiny yarn: for the final contours of the face and chest.

- Small plastic eyes.

EMBROIDERY

FRONT

1. Beak: pom-pom.
2. Hat: pom-pom.
3. Hat contour: loops.
4. Fine white stripes in scarf: stem stitch.
5. Wider light blue stripes in scarf: loops.
6. Scarf: fringe.
7. Face and tummy: flat stitch.
8. Face and tummy contours: flat stitch.

BACK

9. Hat: pom-pom.
10. Fine white stripes in scarf: stem stitch.
11. Wider light blue stripes in scarf: loops.
12. Body: flat stitch.

EXTRAS

- Make a pom-pom for the hat.

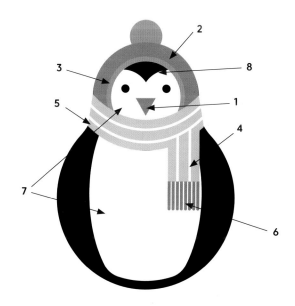

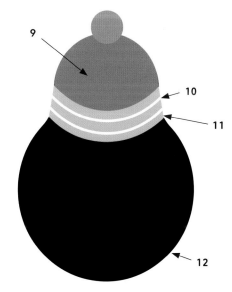

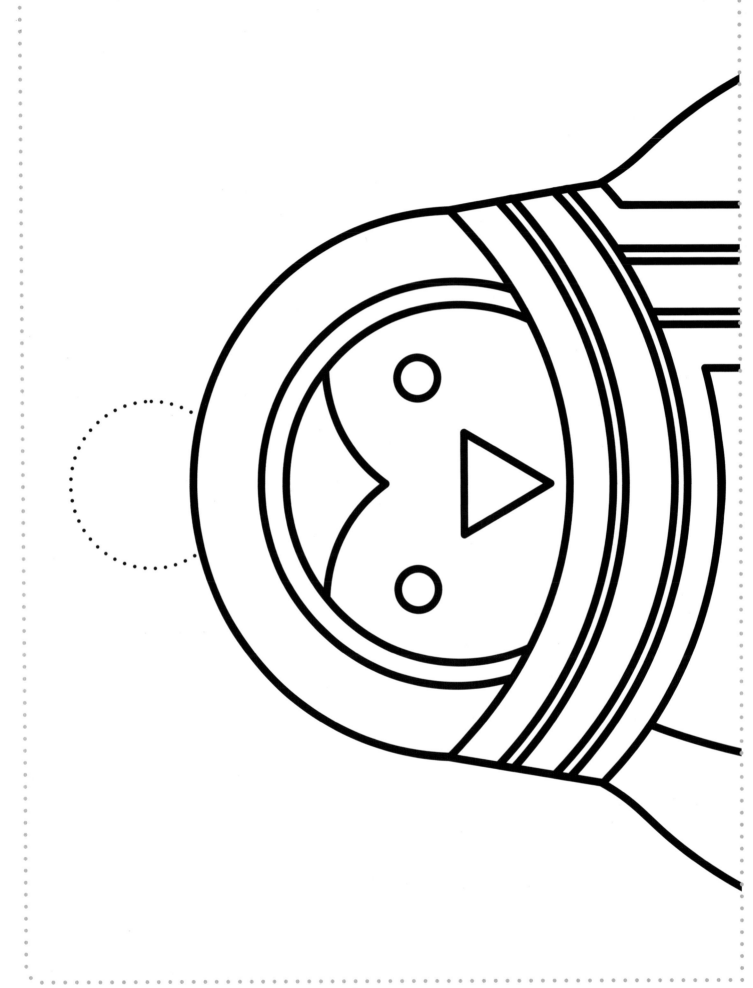

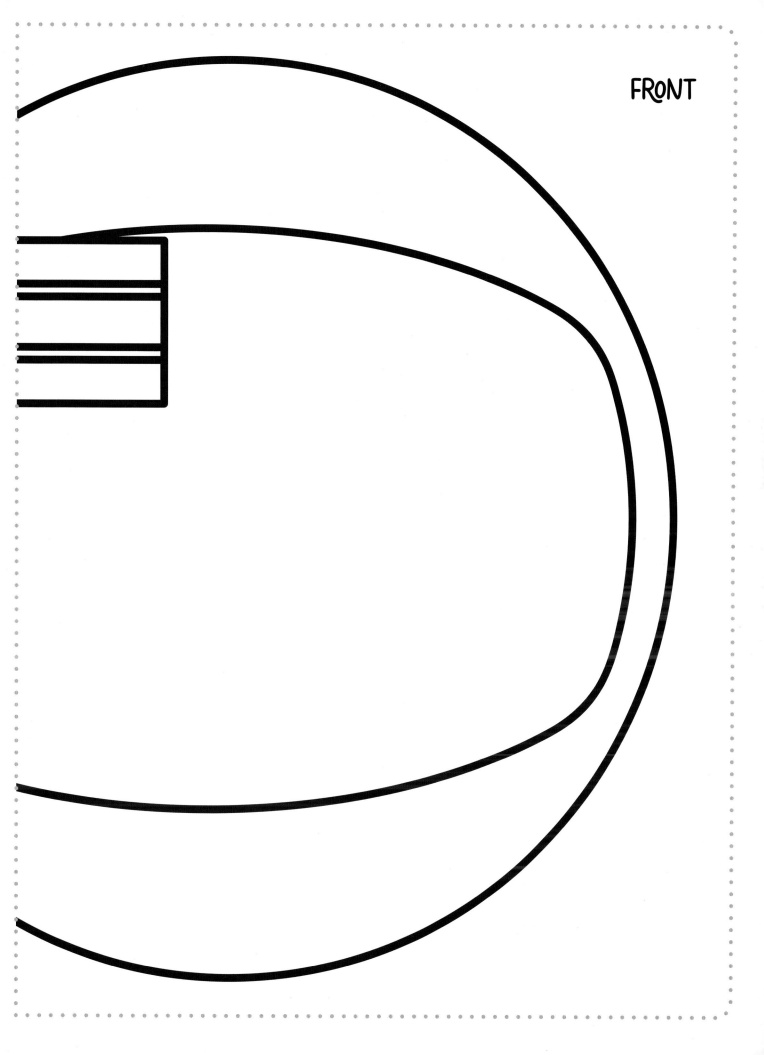

FRONT

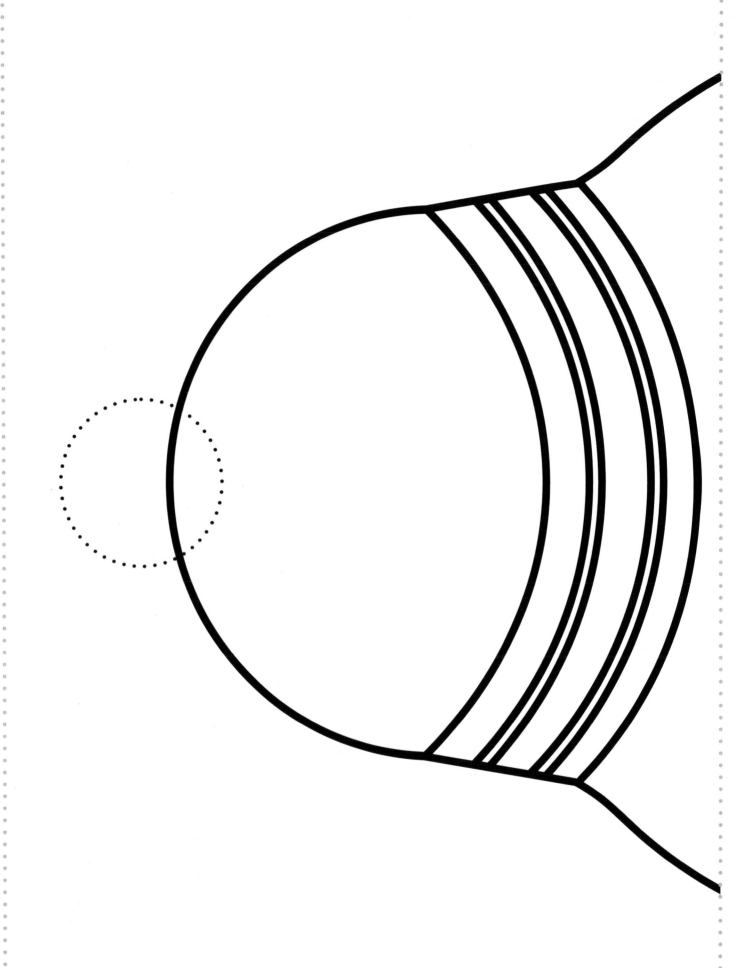

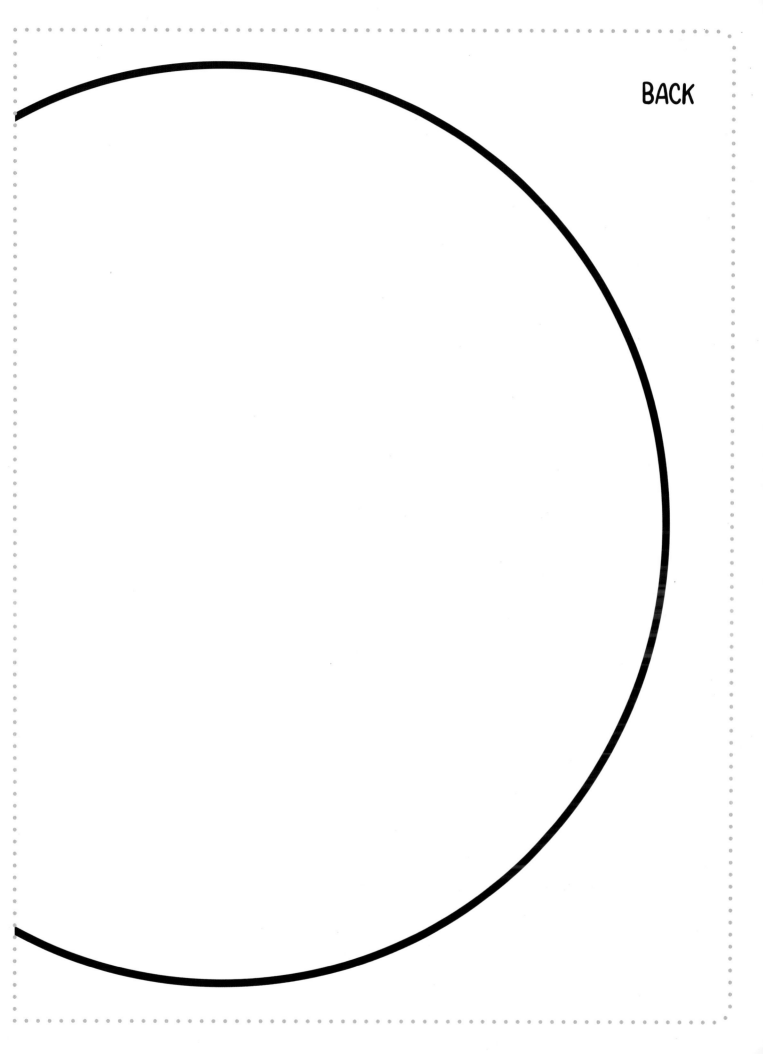

BACK

PEDRO PIG

If this is the first time you've seen Pedro, you might feel a bit scared and intimidated by his eye patch and tattoos. He has a look that says, 'Don't mess with me', but when you get to know him, you'll see that he is a nice guy. His skin is his favourite canvas and, despite looking dishevelled, with his half-punk, half-pirate style, Pedro takes care of it with the best body lotions and moisturizers and takes a mud bath once a week to keep his tattoos in top condition. He is always clean and smells good and, if he likes you, he will give you a free tattoo. That's why everyone on the farm has a tattoo but no one has ever paid for them. As I told you, Pedro is a nice guy.

MATERIALS

- Medium punch needle (3mm diameter), 3cm/1⅛in length, for all but the fine details.
- Adjustable fine punch needle (2mm diameter), 4cm/1⅝in length, for the final contours.
- Panama fabric or similar, with 5 holes per cm (⅜in).
- DK (US 3 light, DK, light worsted) yarn: dark pink for the tummy and snout; light pink for the body, ears and hooves; black for the trousers, tattoos and eye patch; blue for the trouser seams.
- Golden embroidery silk or shiny yarn: for the final contours of the tummy.
- Plastic eye.

EMBROIDERY

FRONT

1. Snout: loops.
2. Eye patch and elastic: flat stitch.
3. Tattoo: flat stitch.
4. Tummy: flat stitch.
5. Body and hooves: flat stitch.
6. Waistband: satin stitch.
7. Trouser seams: flat stitch.
8. Trousers: flat stitch.
9. Tummy contours: flat stitch.
10. Tattoos and eye patch elastic: if necessary, redo with flat stitch.

BACK

11. Eye patch elastic: flat stitch.
12. Tattoo: flat stitch.
13. Body and hooves: flat stitch.
14. Waistband: satin stitch.
15. Trouser seams: flat stitch.
16. Trousers: flat stitch.
17. Tattoos and eye patch elastic: if necessary, redo with flat stitch.

EXTRAS

- Embroider ears separately.

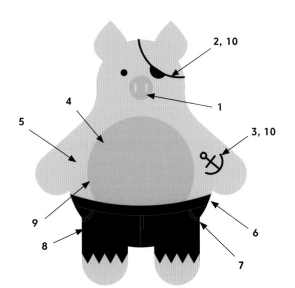
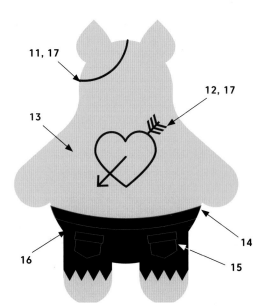

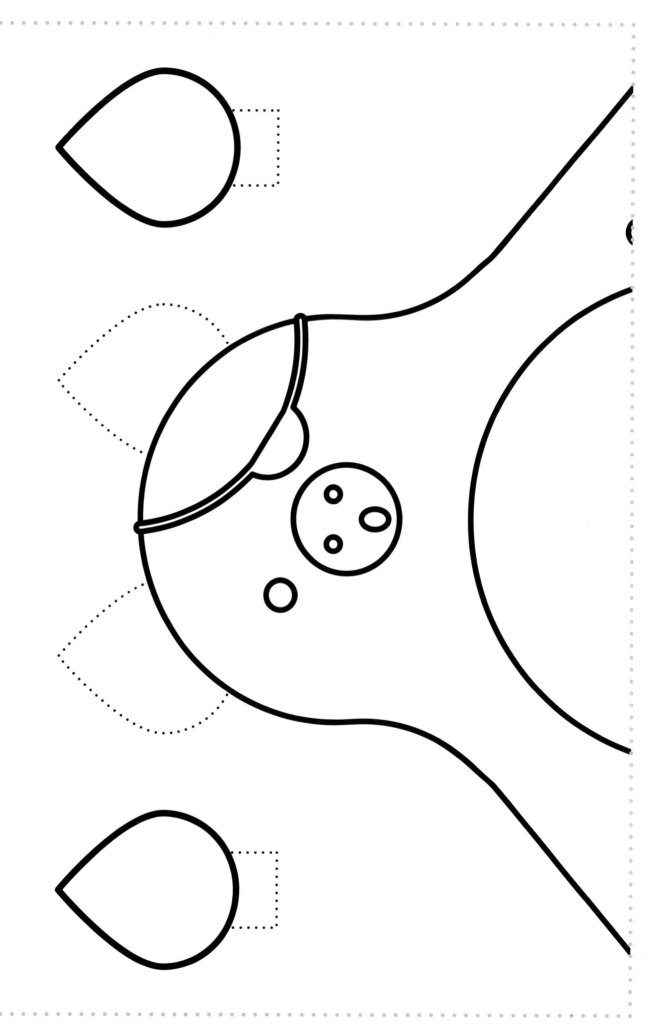

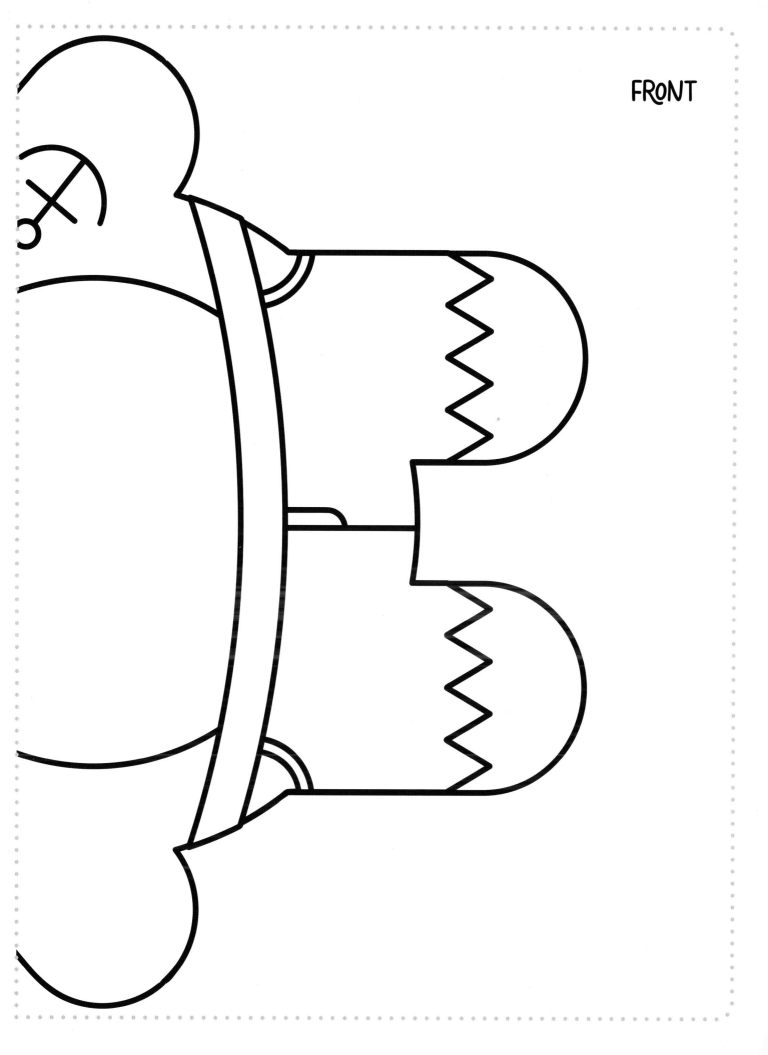

FRONT

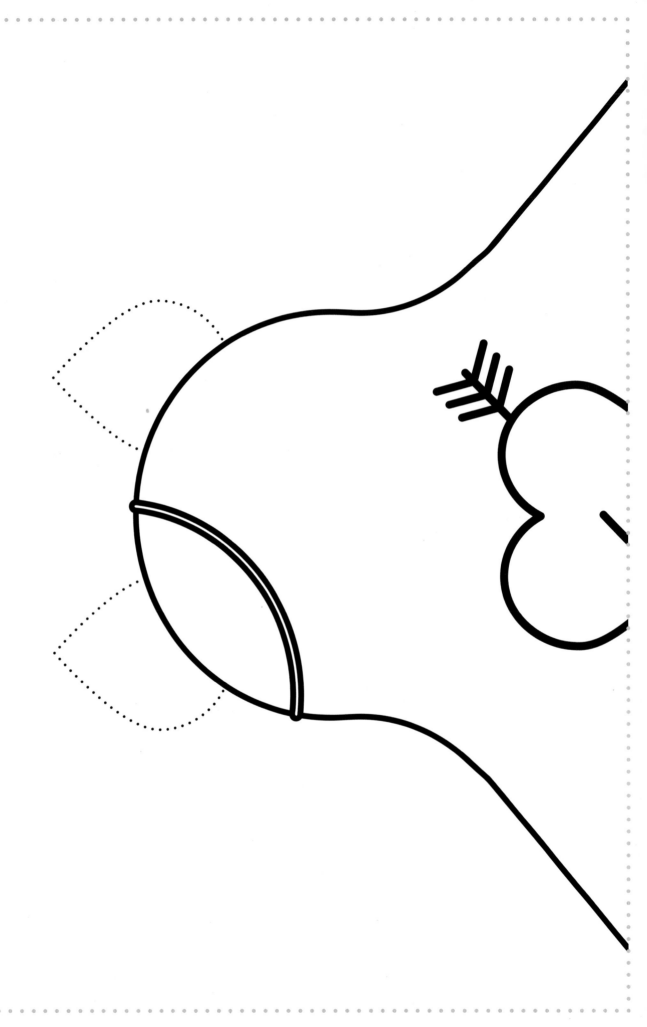

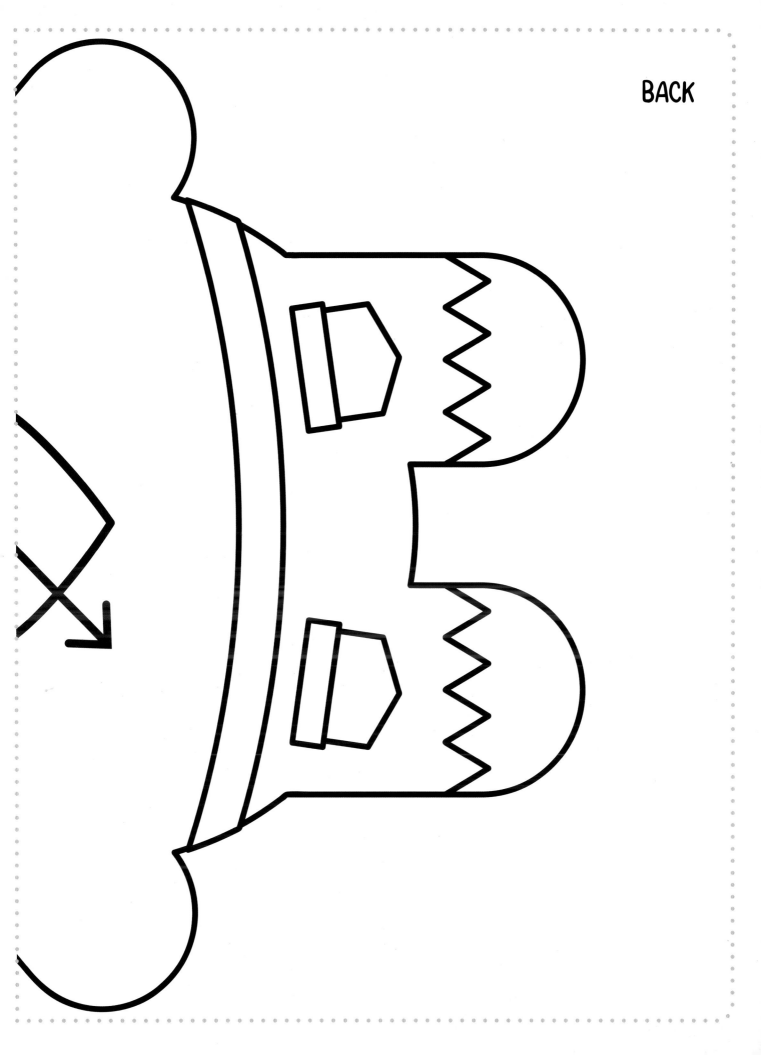

BACK

SIMÓN SLOTH

Simón is what you'd expect of a sloth – he is a sleepyhead. He doesn't like to make any effort, but doesn't like it if others say he's lazy either. He would prefer to be called a 'hedonist'. Somehow, he manages to finish some things or else pretends that he's done them. Once, for the autumn–winter collection of his fashionable clothing brand, he started knitting a sweater, but got tired and didn't finish it, so he presented it as a slipover and said it was intentional. It was an incredible success – all the neighbours wanted to climb trees wearing a yellow slipover like Simón's. He could have sold loads of them, but he wasn't going to interrupt his nap to knit dozens of slipovers, so his was a one-off, super-limited-edition product!

MATERIALS

- Medium punch needle (3mm diameter), 3cm/1⅛in length, for the face and slipover.
- Adjustable fine punch needle (2mm diameter), 3cm/1⅛in length, for the body, claws and final contours.
- Panama fabric or similar, with 5 holes per cm (⅜in).
- DK (US 3 light, DK, light worsted) yarn: dark yellow for the slipover pattern, neck and waist edging; light yellow for the background of the slipover; white and grey for the face.
- 4 ply, baby (US 2 fine, fingering) yarn: brown for the body and paws; white for the claws; black for the mouth.
- Silver embroidery silk or shiny yarn: for the final contours of the face.
- Plastic eyes and nose.

EMBROIDERY

FRONT
1. Body: tufting.
2. Paws: flat stitch.
3. Claws: flat stitch.
4. Mouth: flat stitch.
5. Face: flat stitch.
6. Slipover pattern: thick chain stitch.
7. Slipover pattern: thin chain stitch.
8. Slipover patttern between chains: spike stitch.
9. Slipover pattern centres of spikes: flat stitch line.
10. Slipover, background: flat stitch.
11. Slipover, rhombus pattern: long flat stitches.
12. Slipover neck and waist edging: satin stitch.
13. Slipover neck and waist contours: flat stitch.
14. Face contours: flat stitch.
15. Mouth: if necessary, redo with flat stitch.

BACK
16. Body: tufting.
17. Paws: flat stitch.
18. Claws: flat stitch.
19. Slipover pattern: thick chain stitch.
20. Slipover pattern: thin chain stitch.
21. Slipover pattern between chains: spike stitch.
22. Slipover pattern centres of spikes: flat stitch line.
23. Slipover, background: flat stitch.
24. Slipover neck and waist edging: satin stitch.
25. Slipover neck and waist contours: flat stitch.

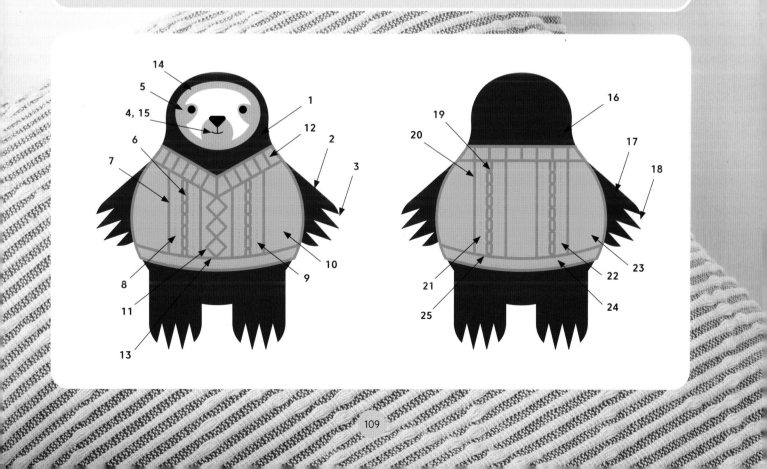

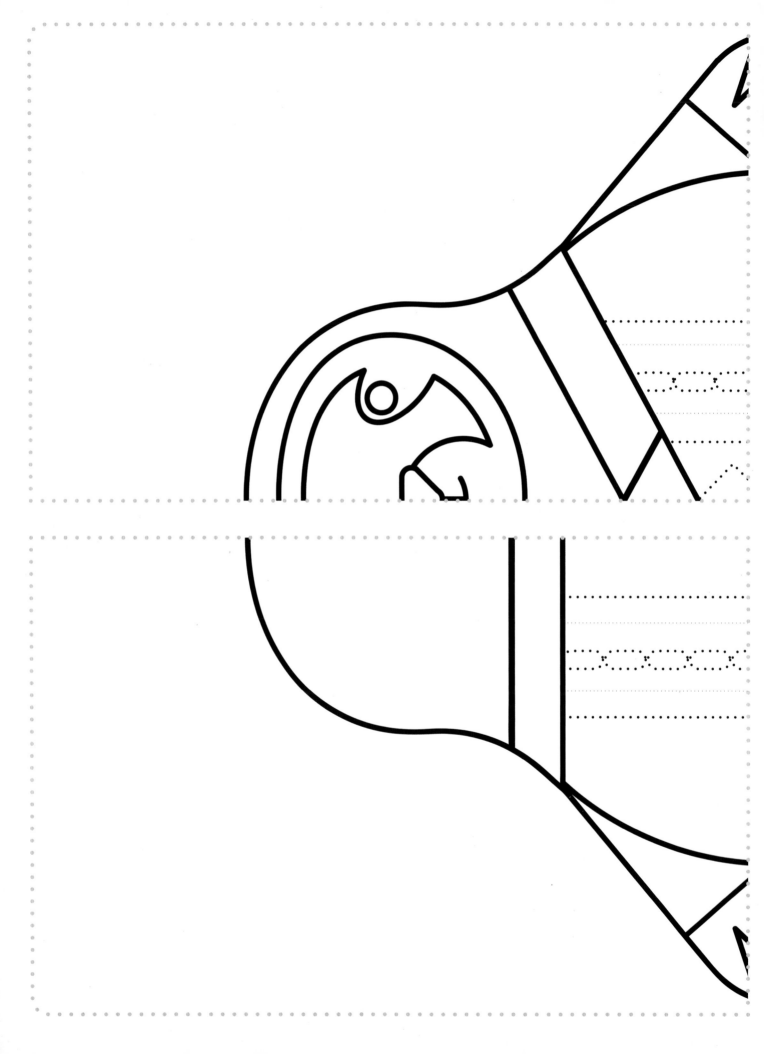

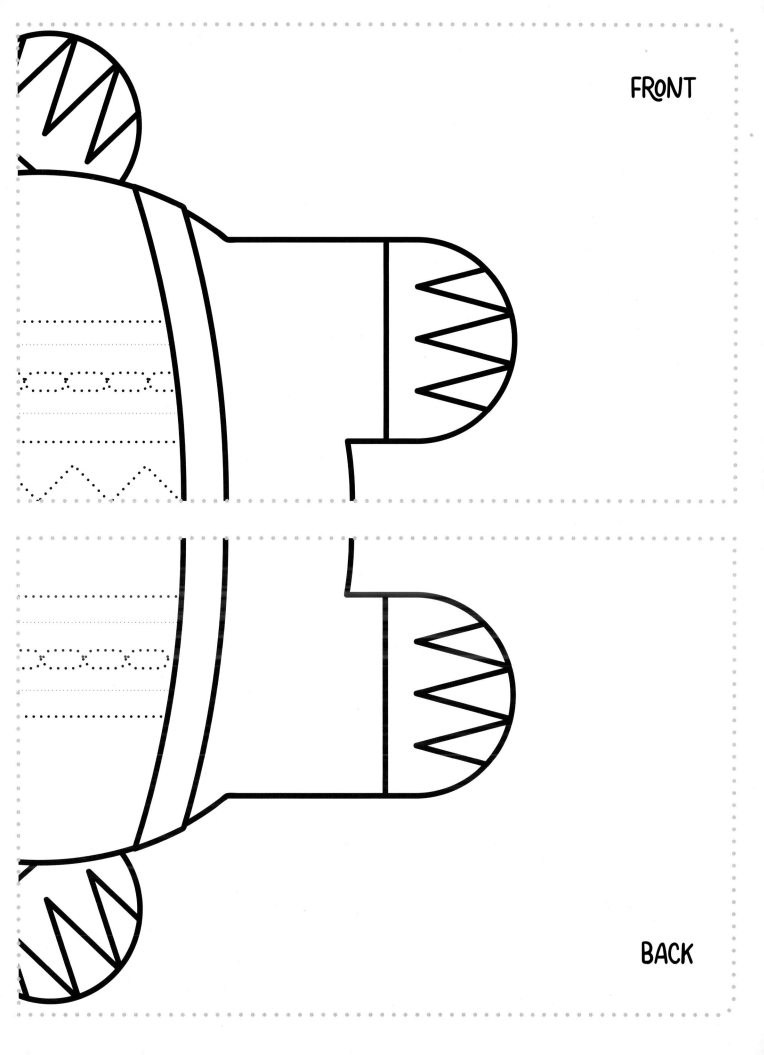

FRONT

BACK

SUSANA SHEEP

Susana never liked to 'follow the herd' and couldn't stand Diego, the sheepdog. 'He thinks he is very clever and orders us about with his barks', she thought. She was the type of sheep that often stopped grazing and went to the other side of the mountain to read historical novels, ignoring Diego's barks calling them to come home. Sometimes Diego lost patience with Susana, but he saw something admirable in her, which is why he let her escape to go to university. When she arrived there after her long journey, in the bottom of her backpack she found a parcel from Diego, gift wrapped and with a card that said, 'This is the only thing that tied you to the farm. Best wishes, Diego'. It was some wool clippers.

MATERIALS

- Extra-thick punch needle (6mm diameter), 4.5cm/1¾in length for Susana's wool.
- Medium punch needle (3mm diameter), 3cm/1⅛in length, for the rest of the toy.
- Adjustable fine punch needle (2mm diameter), 4cm/1⅝in length, for the final contours.
- Open-weave fabric, such as panama, with 4 holes per cm (⅜in).
- Super chunky (US 6 super bulky) yarn: white for Susana's wool.
- DK (US 3 light, DK, light worsted) yarn: grey for the face and ankles; black for the hooves; brown for the hoody.
- Golden embroidery silk or shiny yarn: for the final contours of the hoodie.
- Plastic eyes.

EMBROIDERY

FRONT

1. Fringe: XL loops.
2. Head and lower body: loops.
3. Nose and mouth: flat stitch.
4. Face: flat stitch, worked in a spiral.
5. Ankles and hooves: flat stitch.
6. Hoody pocket: flat stitch, worked in a spiral.
7. Hoody chest: straight flat stitch.
8. Hoody sleeves: straight flat stitch, worked diagonally, following edge of hooves.
9. Letter 'U': flat stitch.
10. Hoody wristbands, waistband and neck opening: satin stitch.
11. Contours: flat stitch.

BACK

12. Head and lower body: loops.
13. Ankles and hooves: flat stitch.
14. Hood: flat stitch, worked in a spiral.
15. Hoody back: straight flat stitch.
16. Hoodie sleeves: straight flat stitch, worked diagonally, following upper edge of front legs.
17. Hoody wristbands and waistband: satin stitch.
18. Contours: flat stitch

EXTRAS

- Hoody cords: using a wool needle, make a long stitch in and out each side of the neck opening and knot each end.
- Embroider ears separately.
- Make a pom-pom for the tail.

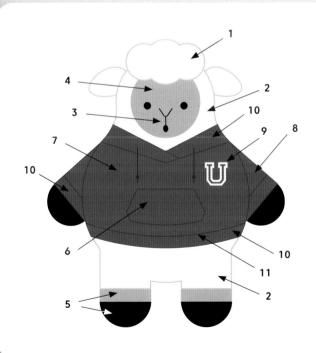

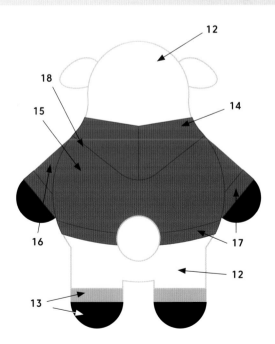

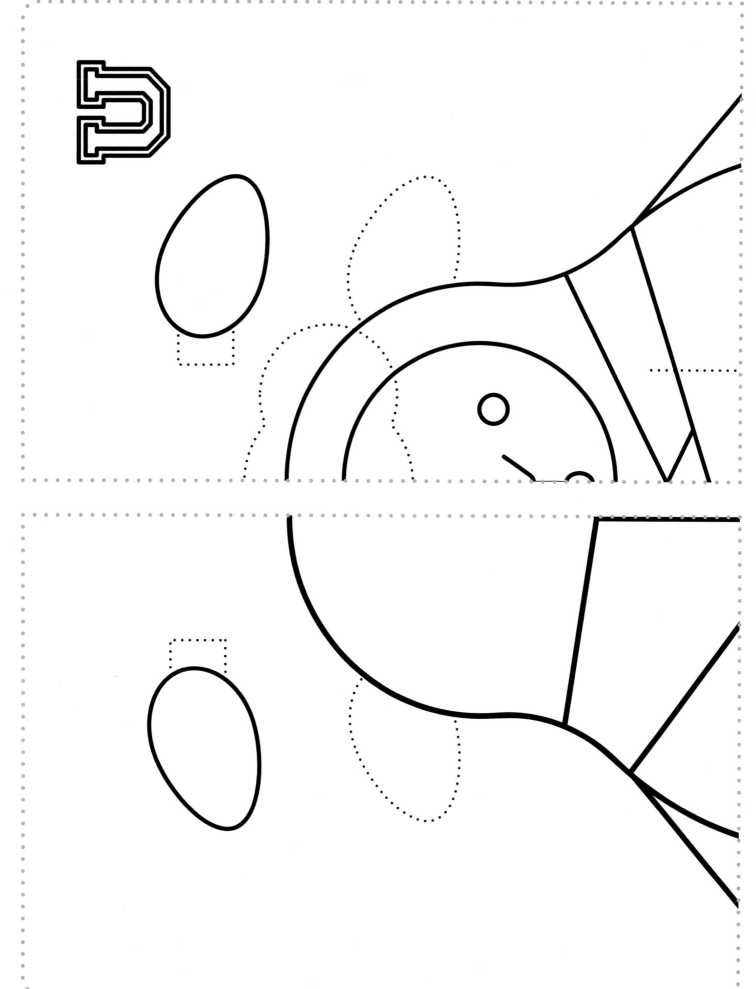

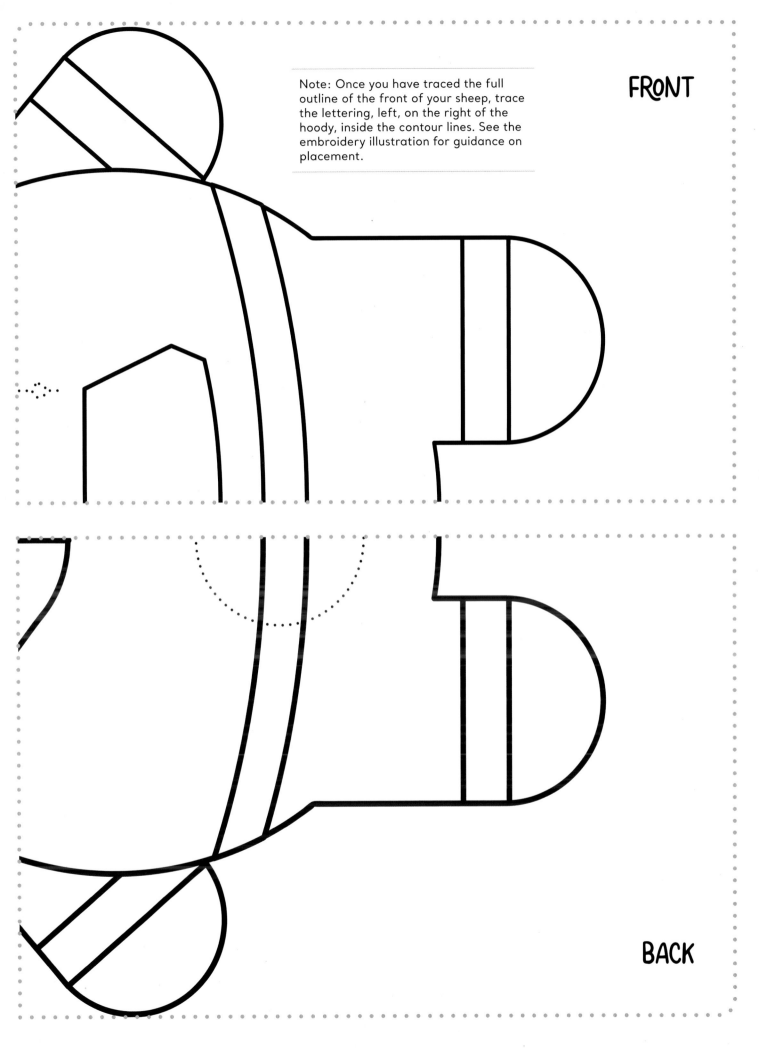

Note: Once you have traced the full outline of the front of your sheep, trace the lettering, left, on the right of the hoody, inside the contour lines. See the embroidery illustration for guidance on placement.

FRONT

BACK

TERESA TORTOISE

Teresa is an architect specializing in interior design. She has applied all her years of experience and knowledge to designing her own home. Inside Teresa's shell is a large, open-plan kitchen, living and dining room, three bathrooms, a main bedroom, guest room, laundry room, even a playroom. As it is physically impossible to go inside a turtle's shell, Teresa created an Instagram account, full of photos of the most beautiful corners of her home, videos of the renovation process and, from time to time, she shares decorating tips with her community. She is now an interiors and lifestyle influencer!

MATERIALS

- Medium punch needle (3mm diameter), 3cm/1⅛in length, for all but the shell and fine details.
- Medium long punch needle (3mm diameter), 6cm/2⅜in length or work XL loops, for the shell.
- Adjustable fine punch needle (2mm diameter), 4cm/1⅝in length, for the final contours.
- Panama fabric or similar, with 5 holes per cm (⅜in).
- DK (US 3 light, DK, light worsted) yarn: green for the skin; light green for the forehead wrinkles; white for the sweater; two shades of brown for the shell.
- Golden embroidery silk or shiny yarn: for the final contours of the sweater.
- Plastic eyes and tiny eyes for nostrils.

EMBROIDERY

FRONT

1. Sweater collar: fill stitch stripes.
2. Sweater pattern: thick chain stitch.
3. Sweater pattern: thin chain stitch.
4. Sweater background: flat stitch.
5. Sweater sleeves: flat stitch.
6. Sweater cable pattern: satin stitch.
7. Forehead wrinkles: flat stitch.
8. Face and legs: flat stitch.
9. Forehead wrinkles: if necessary, redo with flat stitch.
10. Sweater contours: flat stitch

BACK

11. Shell: XL loops.
12. Sweater collar: fill stitch stripes.
13. Sweater sleeves: flat stitch.
14. Head and legs: flat stitch.
15. Sweater contours: flat stitch.

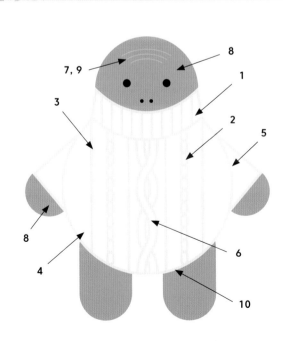

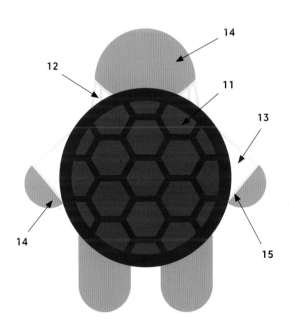

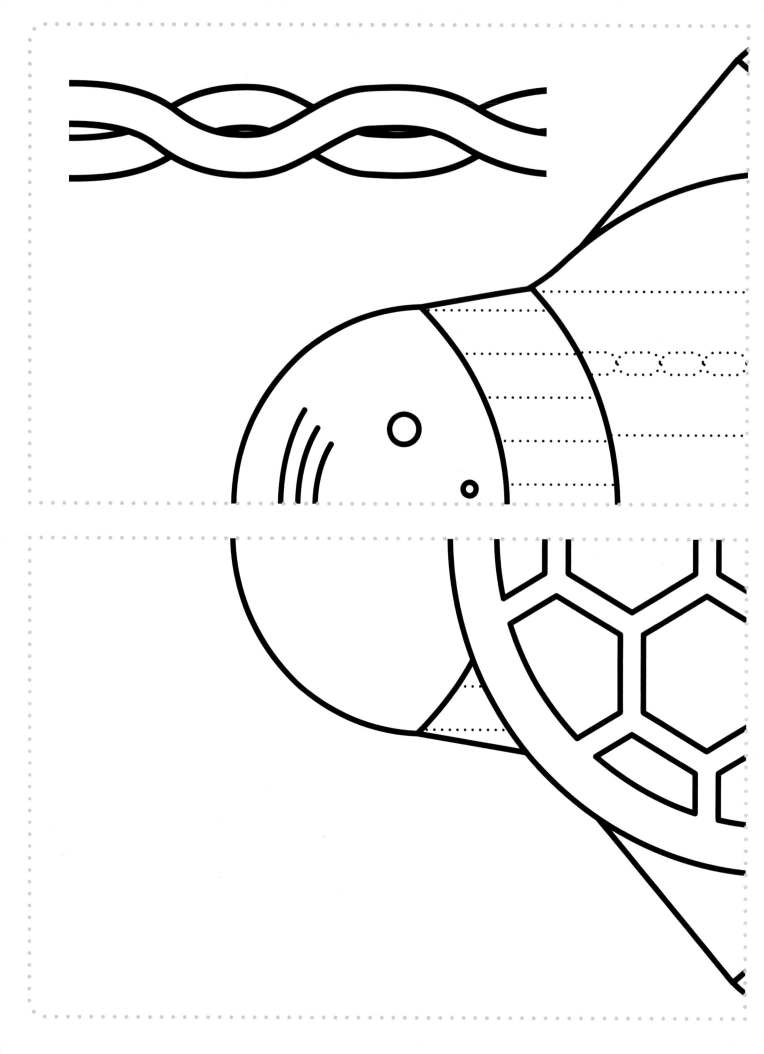

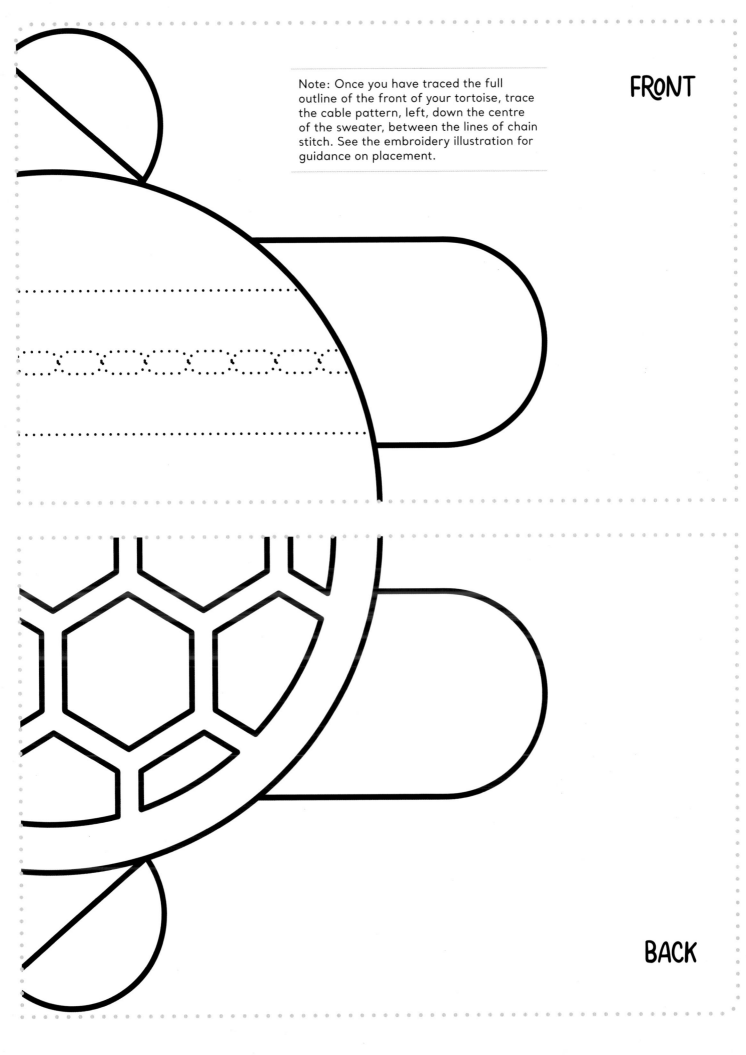

Note: Once you have traced the full outline of the front of your tortoise, trace the cable pattern, left, down the centre of the sweater, between the lines of chain stitch. See the embroidery illustration for guidance on placement.

FRONT

BACK

ZACARÍAS ZEBRA

Zacarías is a supermarket cashier. He likes greeting and helping the customers, but something bothered him a lot. Zacarías's fur drove the barcode reader totally crazy – so much so that, sometimes, customers had to go to the next till while someone came to get the reader working again. One day, Zacarías went to see the manager. He had brought with him his new invention – something called a 'QR code' (yes, he invented it), which has little black squares instead of bars. The manager loved Zacarías's invention so much, he had QR codes printed for all the products in the supermarket. Zacarías made a lot of money from his invention, but is still working in the supermarket. He really enjoys his work.

MATERIALS

- Medium punch needle (3mm diameter), 3cm/1⅛in length, for the apron and nostrils.
- Adjustable fine punch needle (2mm diameter), 2.5cm/1in length, for the fur, hooves and face.
- Adjustable fine punch needle (2mm diameter), 4cm/1⅝in length, for the snout, heart on apron, mane and final contours.
- Panama fabric or similar, with 5 holes per cm (⅜in).
- DK (US 3 light, DK, light worsted) yarn: grey for the nostrils; green for the apron; dark green for the apron edges and straps.
- 4 ply, baby (US 2 fine, fingering) yarn: black for the snout, mane, fur markings, hooves and ears; white for the heart, face and fur markings.
- Silver embroidery silk or shiny yarn: for the decoration lines on the apron.
- Plastic eyes.

EMBROIDERY

FRONT
1. Snout and nostrils: pom-pom.
2. Heart: pom-pom.
3. White fur markings: flat stitch.
4. Black fur markings: flat stitch.
5. Face: flat stitch.
6. Hooves: flat stitch.
7. Apron: flat stitch.
8. Apron edges and straps: satin stitch.
9. Apron decoration lines: flat stitch.

BACK
10. Mane: tufted XL loops.
11. White fur markings: flat stitch.
12. Black fur markings: flat stitch.
13. Hooves: flat stitch.
14. Apron straps: satin stitch.

EXTRAS
- Embroider ears separately.

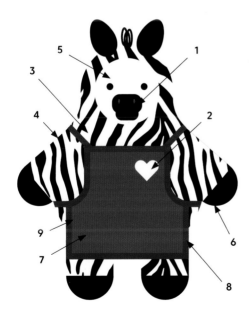

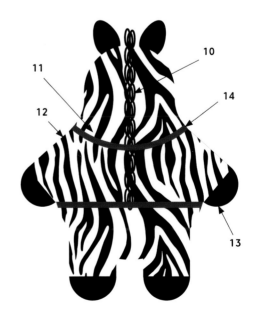

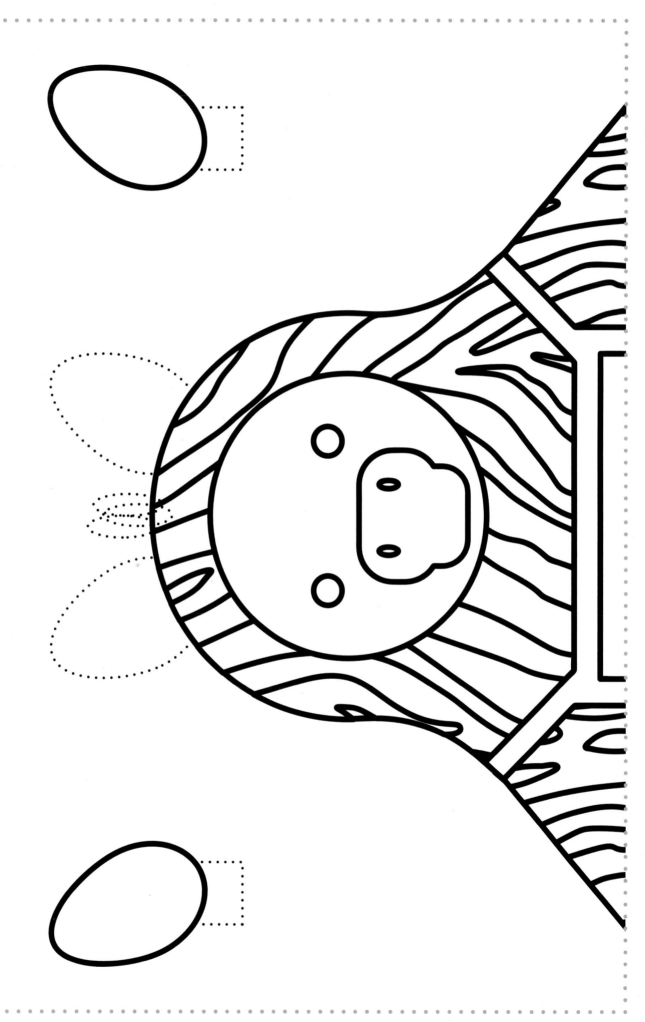

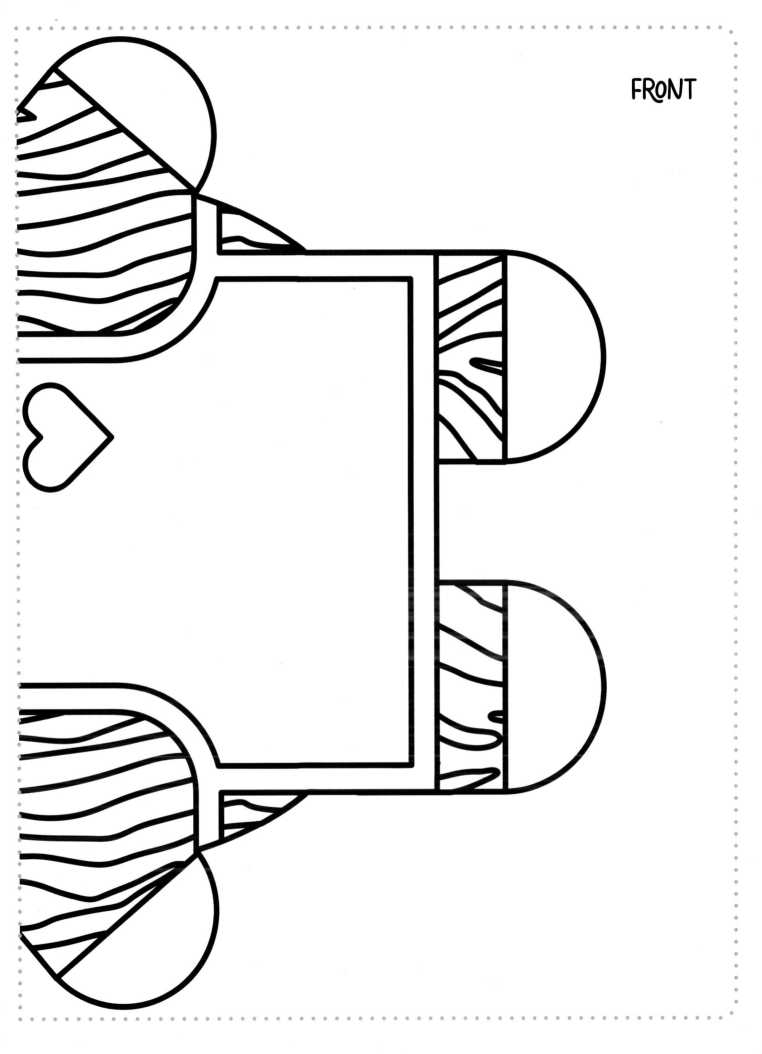

FRONT

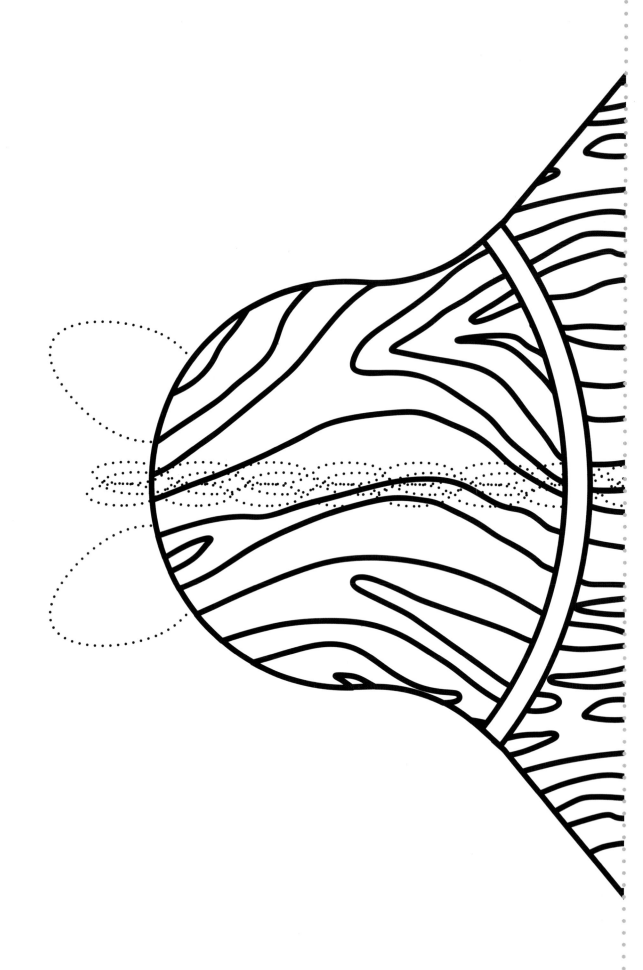

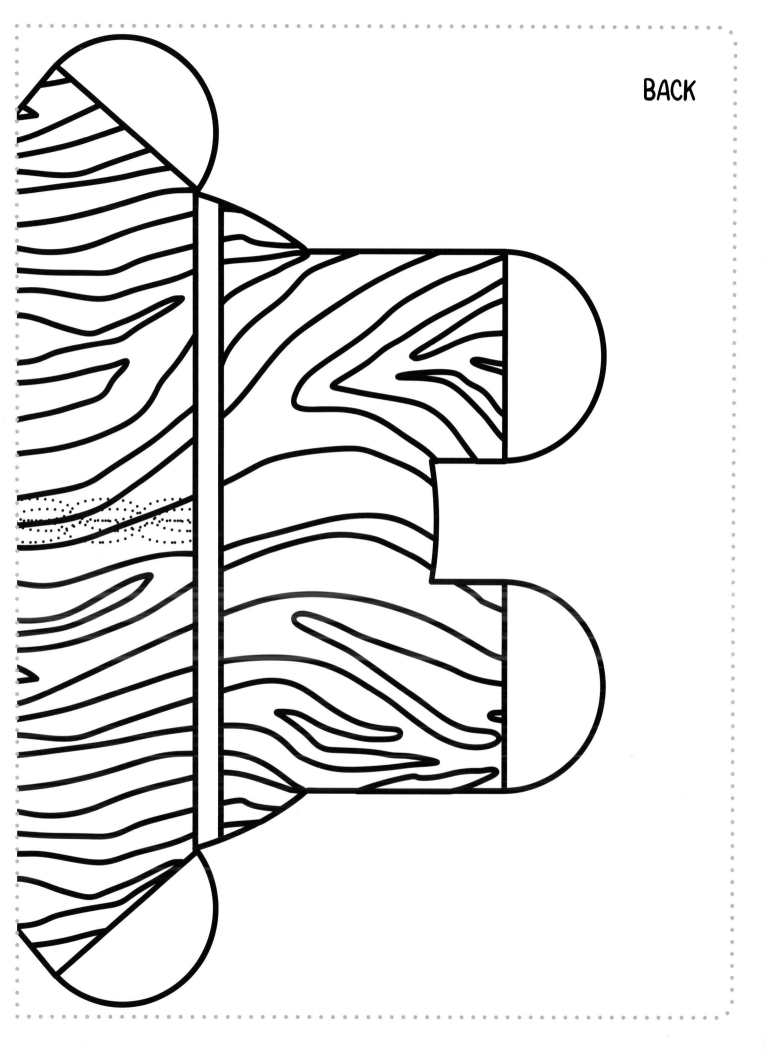

BACK

ABOUT THE AUTHOR

My home city is Buenos Aires, Argentina. In 2011, I graduated with a BA in Graphic Design, then worked as a freelance graphic designer. I also took courses in illustration, photography and pottery, then came across punch needle and loved it! It became my passion, and in 2019 I started to give classes. In 2020, I published my first online course, 'Punch needle XL embroidery' (Doméstika). Thanks to its success, my second course was launched in mid-2021, 'Design and embroidery of dolls with punch needle' (Doméstika).

My pieces have been published in magazines – *Koel*, *Ohlalá*, *Argentina Embroidery Club* and *Rug Hooking* – and exhibited at Casa FOA. I have also participated in photo sessions for the decoration blogs 'Apartment Therapy' and 'Historias de Casa'.

Today I am proud to share my knowledge in this book and encourage you to make the 20 cute embroidered characters, full of colours and textures.

THANKS

To Viviana, my mom, for helping me to make these toys wonderful but, above all, for being the one who introduced me to the world of arts and crafts.

To my dad, Gustavo, for making my best embroidery tools.

And, of course, to Juli, for accompanying me day by day with love and supporting me in all my projects.

126

INDEX

A DAVID AND CHARLES BOOK
© David and Charles, Ltd 2023

David and Charles is an imprint of David and Charles,
Ltd, Suite A, Tourism House, Pynes Hill, Exeter, EX2 5WS

Text and Designs © Caro Bello 2023
Layout and Photography © David and Charles, Ltd 2023

First published in the UK and USA in 2023

A catalogue record for this book is available from the
British Library.

ISBN-13: 9781446309452 paperback
ISBN-13: 9781446382004 EPUB
ISBN-13: 9781446310441 PDF

This book has been printed on paper from approved
suppliers and made from pulp from sustainable sources.

FSC
www.fsc.org
MIX
Paper from
responsible sources
FSC® C012521

Printed in China through Asia Pacific Offset for:
David and Charles, Ltd
Suite A, Tourism House, Pynes Hill, Exeter, EX2 5WS

10 9 8 7 6 5 4 3 2 1

Publishing Director: Ame Verso
Senior Commissioning Editor: Sarah Callard
Managing Editor: Jeni Chown
Project Editor: Michelle Clark
Head of Design: Anna Wade
Design: Lucy Ridley and Jo Langdon
Art Direction: Pru Rogers
Pre-press Designer: Ali Stark
Photography: Jason Jenkins
Production Manager: Beverley Richardson

David and Charles publishes high-quality books on
a wide range of subjects. For more information visit
www.davidandcharles.com.

Share your makes with us on social media using
#dandcbooks and follow us on Facebook and
Instagram by searching for @dandcbooks.

Layout of the digital edition of this book may vary
depending on reader hardware and display settings.